LEICESTER IN 100 DATES

NATASHA SHELDON

First published 2014

The History Press
The Mill, Brimscombe Port
Stroud, Gloucestershire, GL5 2QG
www.thehistorypress.co.uk

British Library Cataloguing in Publication Data.
A catalogue record for this book is available from the British Library.

ISBN 978 0 7524 9921 5

Typesetting and origination by The History Press
Printed in Great Britain

Contents

Acknowledgements

The author wishes to express her gratitude to the the staff at Leicester Record Office.

And to Neil, for the gift of time.

Introduction

You may not think it, but Leicester is an ancient city. One of the oldest in Britain, in fact.

Stretching back beyond the housing estates, shopping complexes, sports stadiums, offices and roads is a long history, dating to the Romans and beyond. Here you will find the Ratae Corieltauvorum, 'the walled place of the Coritani', the settlement of the local Celtic tribe whose lands around the River Soar became a substantial Roman municipal city, some of which remains today. Then comes the Leicester of the Saxons, Danes and Vikings, who alternately built and destroyed the town and left their mark on many of the modern street names. The Leicester of the Middle Ages was a thriving market town, whose guilds constructed its finest remaining medieval building, the guildhall, and whose castle played host to kings and parliaments – and saw its fair share of destruction.

Evidence of the wealth brought to the town by the Industrial Revolution is all around, in the remains of hosiery factories and the grand civic buildings of the Victorian period. But Leicester was also a town of innovators: radicals and reformers who may not have made their mark physically on the fabric of the town, but did help shape it in other, more subtle ways.

Each of these different phases of Leicester's life have acted as building blocks, slowly constructing the modern, multicultural city we know today. Trying to find 100 days to represent the historical building project that is Leicester is a difficult task, not least because there are so many to choose from!

It is made somewhat easier by the fact that some events simply cannot be included, because they cannot be dated. So it is not possible to include interesting and important events such as the construction of the Roman forum, the recapture of Leicester from the Danes by Aethelflaed, daughter of Alfred the Great, or Simon de Montfort's expulsion of the Jews from his half of the honour of Leicester (only for his aunt to give them sanctuary on her share of the honour) because there are no exact dates for these events.

But what can be included are 100 of the datable events from Leicester's history that will hopefully show how the past and the present of this fascinating town connect. Each 'brick' is included not only to describe the great moments of Leicester's life and its role in history, but also the smaller events that give a feeling for the character of the town and its people. They will show not only how certain things have evolved over time helping with an understanding of modern Leicester but also how, in terms of human experience, so much ultimately stays the same.

LEICESTER
IN 100 DATES

22 February

After the Battle of Hastings, the manor of Leicester, along with 100 others – sixty-five of them in Leicestershire – were awarded to Hugh de Grandmesnil, a close companion and major supporter of William the Conqueror. De Grandmesnil became Leicester's earl and its sheriff and settled down to make improvements to his new town.

In 1080, he repaired Leicester Castle and its adjoining church of St Mary de Castro. The improved castle defences came in particularly useful when, after King William's death, de Grandmesnil came under attack because of his support for Duke Robert against the new king, William Rufus.

But de Grandmesnil survived and on this day in 1094, Leicester's first Norman earl died at Leicester Castle. Yet, despite having lived out so much of his life in England, the earl's heart belonged to Normandy and that was precisely where he wanted his earthly remains to lie. On his death, his body was preserved in salt and sewn up in an ox hide. It was then sent back to Normandy, where it was buried on the south side of the chapter house of St Evroul. His wife had already made the journey at her death and so de Grandmesnil was buried at her side.

28 July

Today, Leicester was 'dismantled to wear the badge of its owner's disobedience'.

Robert Blanchemains, Earl of Leicester, was a chief supporter of Queen Eleanor and her children in their rebellion against King Henry II. Leicester became a 'chief refuge for the disaffected', so, on 4 July, the king's forces besieged the town in an attempt to break the earl's power.

Robert was captured at Bury St Edmunds and taken prisoner. But still Leicester held out. According to contemporary chronicler Matthew Paris, the Saxon townspeople were 'obliged' to fight by the earl's Norman soldiers, rather than from any loyalty to their lord. Either way, it did them little good. When the King's High Justiciary, Richard de Lucy, finally breached Leicester's walls, the earl's soldiers retreated to the castle to make a last stand, leaving the people of Leicester to fight for their survival.

Leicester burned as the king's men 'fired' the town. What they did not burn was destroyed by 'force of men and engines'. Finally, when the town walls were destroyed, the people surrendered. They bought their lives with £300 worth of silver, but many were also exiled from Leicester as punishment for their resistance. Some parishes were so conclusively destroyed that orchards, rather than houses, covered the land for many years to come.

26 December

The Portmanmoot was the town council of Leicester. Pre-Norman in origin, it was composed of twenty-four prominent townsmen, or jurats, presided over by the alderman (a precursor of the mayor). The Portmanmoot punished crime, controlled trade and commerce and effectively administered the town.

But its powers were limited by its obligations to its lord and the king – until today, for King John issued a royal charter, giving the Portmanmoot unprecedented powers and freedoms to trade and deal in land. The charter granted 'to the burgesses of the town of Leicester that they may go and come freely and without hindrance and may trade through all our land with all things and with their merchandise' and that 'all purchases and sales of lands of the town of Leicester which are and which shall be made reasonably in the portmanmoot of the town shall remain firm and stable'.

No other town in England received such freedoms until the signing of Magna Carta. But Leicester's privileges were given for a reason and came with a price. For while the king was giving up his right to a share in any deals the Portmanmoot might make, it had to pay him a 'fee farm' or yearly 'rent' for the freehold of the town, therefore guaranteeing John much-needed income for his military endeavours.

22 October

Today a law was passed which revolutionised the method of inheritance in Leicester. Up until this point, the town had practiced ultimogeniture, or the 'Borough English' method of inheritance. This meant that the youngest son or daughter inherited, rather than the eldest as in the growing Norman practice of primogeniture.

Ultimogeniture was also the method of inheritance commonly practised amongst unfree peasants and villeins. The elder children would usually leave home to make their own way in the world, leaving younger siblings to care for their elderly parents, and so inherit from them.

The pride of the Burgesses of Leicester no doubt suffered from the indignity of being obliged to pass on their property like peasants, while their neighbours in Nottingham inherited according to the French system of primogeniture. But ultimogeniture was also damaging. In practice, it meant splitting inheritances between all offspring, not just the youngest, impoverishing estates and so weakening businesses in Leicester.

So the burgesses petitioned their earl, Simon de Montfort, for a change in the law and on this day he was able to oblige. He secured a royal sanction to allow the eldest son to inherit 'for the improvement of the state of the town which on account of the feebleness and youthfulness of the heirs for a long time past has almost fallen into ruin and decay'.

26 December

An extract from the borough records relates an incident from this night in 1300 that illustrates the dangerous state of the streets of medieval Leicester after dark.

On this, St Stephen's Day, a William of Loughborough was out walking late along a lane near St Martin's church. It was some hours after curfew, so William should have been at home. But he was not the only one who was on the streets when he should not have been. While walking near the church, he encountered a man named Adam, a servant of a Lady Pitchford, who was accompanied by Richard Smith of Leicester.

Whether the three already knew each other and what exactly transpired between them is not recorded. But Adam and Richard Smith were armed and as a result of a quarrel, fuelled by Christmas drink or perhaps an attempt at robbery, Adam shot William of Loughborough through the back with a barbed arrow.

Adam immediately fled the scene in a panic, while for some inexplicable reason, a much cooler-headed Richard Smith lingered long enough to slice off the fingers of the still-living William's left hand.

William lived through his ordeal 'until the third hour', long enough to make it home to his wife, tell his tale and receive the last rites.

2 November

In the fourteenth century, the heretical Lollards were a growing threat to the authority of the Church. Looking to the scriptures rather than priests for guidance, they denied the Eucharist was the body of Christ and dismissed the validity of the images of the saints and church relics. Most damning of all, they undermined the authority of the clergy by insisting that lay people could also preach and teach.

The problem was of sufficient cause for concern for the Archbishop of Canterbury, William Courteney, to summon an ecclesiastic court at Leicester Abbey on 1 November 1389. A number of Leicester citizens – Roger Dexter, Nicholas Taylor, Richard Wagstaff, Michael Scrivener, William Smith, John Henry, William Parchmener and Roger Goldsmith – were charged with Lollardy. They did not appear and so were found guilty and excommunicated in their absence.

The condemned Lollards went into hiding in Leicester, so measures had to be taken to ensure the town gave them up for exile or repentance. So on this day, the archbishop laid the whole town under an interdict: until the fugitives were found, the people of Leicester were denied Christian offices. No church services could be held in the town and the people could not be attended to by a priest – denying them crucial sacraments such as the last rites and funerals.

3 February

Today, John of Gaunt, Earl of Leicester and Duke of Lancaster, died at Leicester Castle, reputedly his favourite of the thirty residences in his duchy.

The duchy was so vast that it was virtually an independent state within England. This made John of Gaunt – a son of Edward III, uncle to the then king, Richard II, and the richest nobleman in England – a force to be reckoned with.

Many attribute the 'time-honoured Lancastrian's' death at just 58 to grief over the exile of his son, Henry Bolingbroke. Bolingbroke had quarrelled with Thomas Mowbray, Duke of Norfolk, who had accused him of treasonous remarks. The king had exiled Henry but supposedly remained on friendly terms with his uncle. He reputedly visited the duke during his illness bearing a bundle of documents and, although they conversed amicably, after reading the papers John took a turn for the worse and died soon afterwards. Others, however, state that the three-times married notorious womaniser was killed by a venereal disease.

But whatever the cause of John's death, it became the ultimate trigger in the deposition of one king and the ascension of another. On his uncle's death, Richard deprived his errant cousin of his inheritance, causing Bolingbroke to invade England, overthrow Richard and proclaim himself Henry IV.

30 April

On this day, during the reign of Henry V, a parliament began in Leicester, which secured the rights of the commons – and disenfranchised heretics. It became known as the 'Fire and Faggot Parliament'.

The parliament met at Le Fermerier, part of the Greyfriars priory. Here, the commons moved to further secure their rights. They petitioned to have their right to remain a perpetual part of future parliaments recognised and moved that no law would be made without their agreement. But the king's uncle, the Bishop of Winchester, also raised the question of the continuing problem of Lollardism and other heresies. He proposed that anyone found guilty of such crimes should be deprived of their property.

Known as the Suppression of Heresy Act, the bill moved against 'whoever should read the Scriptures in English' – a central tenant of Lollardism – and stipulated that any such person 'should forfeit land, cattle, goods, and life, and be condemned as heretics to God, enemies to the Crown, and traitors to the kingdom; that they should not have the benefit of any sanctuary, though this was a privilege then granted to the most notorious malefactors; and that, if they continued obstinate, or relapsed after pardon, they should first be hanged for treason against the king, and then burned for heresy against God'.

18 February

At just 4 years old, King Henry VI was not old enough to rule in his own right. Unfortunately, this led to a struggle for power between the Chancellor of England, Henry Beaufort, Bishop of Winchester, and the young king's uncle and protector, Humphrey, Duke of Gloucester.

When the king's elder uncle, John, Duke of Bedford, returned from France, he called a parliament to resolve the squabble between the bishop and Gloucester. Armed confrontation between the two factions had already occurred on London Bridge the previous October, so Bedford chose Leicester as a neutral spot, well away from the tensions of the capital.

But violence threatened to spill over into the parliament and so it fell to the duke, as the king's commissioner, to control the tension. To this end, he ordered that no one attending the parliament could enter carrying arms.

Using typical political guile, instead of bringing their swords, the politicians and their men hid stones and lumps of lead up their long sleeves, as well as staves and wooden bats that could be used as weapons, giving the parliament the name of the 'Parliament of Bats'.

But despite this less-than-promising start, not a bat was swung nor a stone thrown during the sessions at Leicester Castle. Indeed, on 7 March, the two protagonists at last reached a peaceful agreement.

5 May

As its earl was also the Earl of Lancaster, it was natural that the town of Leicester should be a loyal supporter of the House of Lancaster during the Wars of the Roses. But in 1462, the town's loyalties shifted when Leicester forces came to the aid of the House of York.

On this day, newly crowned Yorkist King Edward IV showed his gratitude for that support when, at a ceremony at Leicester Castle, he rewarded the mayor, Robert Rawlett, and the two parliamentary burgesses, Thomas Green and John Roberd, with an annuity.

The charter bestowed a grant of 20 marks per year (approximately £13 6s 8d) for the next twenty years to the town officials 'in consideration of the good and faithful and unpaid service which the Mayor and Burgesses of our town of Leicester have cheerfully rendered of late in our behalf against our enemies hostilely raising war against us as also of the heavy burden of their no small losses incurred touching such business of ours'.

The gratitude of the king to the Leicester officials for their support must have been deep indeed. Two years later, when Edward was withdrawing many similar grants from other towns in order to save money, he did not rescind the Leicester annuity.

22 August

Only a day after leaving Leicester at the head of an army thought to be heading for certain victory at Bosworth Field, the body of Richard III was returned to the town in very different circumstances.

According to Polydore Vergil, a contemporary chronicler, the evening after the battle, Henry Tudor retraced Richard's steps, leading his victorious forces to Leicester. In their midst was the corpse of Richard III.

The fallen Yorkist king's return to Leicester was very different from his dignified exit. Then, he was crowned and in armour. Now, any onlookers would have seen a filthy, bound and naked corpse slung like baggage over the saddle of a horse, with matted hair and blood obscuring its face. But besides the wounds of battle, they would have seen the signs of Richard's enemies' spite – the 'humiliation wounds' commonly visited on the bodies of fallen foes, which in Richard's case were visible on his buttocks.

The procession made its way over the Bow Bridge, the West Bridge and into the town via its west gate. From there, it made its way to the Newarke, where a final humiliation awaited the dead king: his body was publicly displayed in the Church of the Annunciation of the Blessed Virgin – the Lancastrian faction's preferred burial site.

21 September

On 2 July 1489, King Henry VII decided that too many 'persons of little substance and reason' who 'contributed little to the public purse' were involved in the town council of Leicester. So he issued a mandate to the town's mayor and burgesses, which stated that from then on only forty-eight 'wise and sad commoners' chosen by the town officials could be present at common halls and assemblies. Of the whole town of Leicester, only those forty-eight people could take part in council elections. With that, Henry effectively banned most of Leicester from having a say in the running of the town.

The mayor and burgesses accepted the ruling readily enough, but the people of Leicester were having none of it. Today, in defiance of the king, they rejected the mayor elected by the forty-eight, Roger Tryng, and held their own elections, selecting instead a man called Thomas Toutheby.

Henry was not pleased with this defiance of his ruling, but the town escaped lightly enough. To smooth things out, the king reinstated the original mayor at the time of the ruling, Thomas Davy, and made his tenure official under the privy seal just to be on the safe side. But Thomas Toutheby was punished – Henry permanently barred him from taking part in the town's assemblies.

HENRY VII

16 May

It was customary in medieval times for wealthy men to undertake good works for the benefit of their souls. On 13 July 1513, Henry VIII granted a license to one such good work in Leicester – Wyggeston's Hospital. On this day, the hospital was completed and handed over to its master chaplain, William Fisher, to prepare for the first residents.

Founded by wealthy Leicester wool merchant William Wyggeston, the 'hospital' was situated on land along Friar Lane and St Martin's churchyard. It was not founded as an infirmary for the sick but rather as an almshouse for the elderly poor of Leicester. Under the terms of the license, Wyggeston was granted the right to 'create, erect and establish a perpetual hospital of 2 perpetual chaplains and twelve perpetual poor folk ... Men, blind, lame, decrepit, paralytic, or maimed in their limbs, and idiots wanting their natural senses'.

The inmates were to be unmarried and without other support. By the time the hospital was ready to open, provision had also been made for twelve women, 'poor, aged, and of good report and honest conversation'.

Attended by two chaplains and attendants, the able-bodied residents were expected to care for the most infirm residents. And although the hospital has since moved site, Wyggeston's hospital continues to care for the elderly of Leicester today.

29 November

On this day, the disgraced prelate and former first minister of Henry VIII, Cardinal Thomas Wolsey, died at Leicester Abbey. Stripped of his offices after failing to secure Henry a divorce from Catherine of Aragon, Wolsey had been effectively exiled in York, having already surrendered all of his property to the king. But in the autumn of 1530, he was charged with treason and summoned to London.

The journey was a hard one for Wolsey. He was described as 'so sick that he was divers times likely to have fallen from his mule'. When he finally arrived at the gates of Leicester Abbey on 26 November, a welcoming torch-lit party of the abbot and his monks met him. The cardinal is reputed to have said, 'Father Abbot, I am come hither to leave my bones amongst you.'

Once in his room, the cardinal took to his bed, where he stayed, becoming 'sicker and sicker' (with diarrhoea, amongst other things), until he passed away on this night at around 8 p.m. The abbot immediately called the Mayor of Leicester and the aldermen to view the body, which was dressed in its full vestments. But at the time of his death, the cardinal was wearing the hair shirt of a penitent – a sign that he knew his end was near, whether on the road or in London.

28 August

Despite outlasting many of the other abbeys of England, the Abbey of Saint Mary de Pratis at Leicester was surrendered by the last abbot, John Bourchier, to Dr Francis Care, Cromwell's commissionaire on this date.

The Augustan Abbey was founded in the twelfth century by the 2nd Earl of Leicester, Robert le Bossu, and had been the wealthiest religious establishment in Leicestershire as well as one of the most important Augustan houses in England. It owed its long survival after the initial reformation to the fact that Abbot Bourchier was a nominee installed by Cromwell in 1534, no doubt to ensure a smooth Dissolution.

Bourchier, however, did his best to save the abbey. He persuaded its canons to accept Henry VIII's supremacy of the Church of England and reduced its debts from £1,000 a year to just £441. With an income of £951 14s 5¾d by the time of its surrender, St Mary's was actually profitable again. The abbot also made presents to Cromwell of money and livestock. But it was all in vain. For although one of Cromwell's spies, Richard Layton, reported Bourchier honest, he condemned the canons as adulterous and unnatural – possibly because they objected to Bourchier's intention to lease the manor of Ingarsby to Richard Cromwell.

Dr Care quickly demolished the abbey completely, selling it off as building materials.

9 March

On 19 February, a Leicester man called Kettle was convicted of treason against Queen Mary I at the Leicester spring assizes. His execution was fixed for this date.

The exact details of the charge remain mysterious. It is possible that Kettle was involved in Wyatt's Rebellion, which involved Sir Thomas Wyatt and Henry Grey, 1st Duke of Suffolk. The aim was to dethrone the increasingly unpopular Mary and replace her with her half-sister Elizabeth.

Whatever the details, the trial was significant enough for Henry Hastings, 3rd Earl of Huntingdon (acting as the Queen's Witness), to attend and for Kettle to be prosecuted by the Queen's Solicitor, the name sadly lost to history, in person. The court sentenced Kettle to be hanged, drawn and quartered. The town accounts reveal how two men were stationed in the steeple of St Martin's church to announce the arrival of the Earl of Huntingdon, who was attending as the Queen's Witness. The town itself was heavily secured, the four gates strengthened and guards issued with armour.

The gallows were erected at the High Cross, just outside the town walls. The accounts show that the undersheriff, a Mr Berridge, supervised the matter. He was paid 10s for 'such things as was done about the execution of Kettle and setting up his head and quarters'. The quarters were set over each of the town gates, while Kettle's head was probably fitted to the High Cross itself.

21 April

The reign of Mary I was a dangerous time for Protestant dissenters and it was unwise to express any such views openly, even in a provincial town like Leicester. For one young man, a visit with friends in Leicester led to his trial for heresy on this day.

A local merchant employed 24-year-old Thomas Moore who, while in a church with some friends, was overheard to say that statues of saints were empty idols and that his god was in heaven, not in the vessel containing the Eucharist. Denying the sacrament was a sure sign of Protestantism and so Thomas Moore was reported to the authorities.

Moore was summoned to appear before the visiting Bishop of Lincoln, Dr John White, in St Margaret's church. The bishop asked him what he saw before him on the altar of the church, referring to the pyx, containing the sacramental wafer. More replied that he saw the altar ornaments. The bishop then asked him if the 'blood, flesh and bones' of Christ were not in the pyx. More replied, 'No'.

This doomed him and he was immediately found guilty of heresy and sentenced to burn. Moore did not recant and on 26 June 1556, the sentence was carried out, which he apparently suffered 'with manly fortitude'.

10 May

The High Cross was an area of ancient significance to the people of Leicester. Marking the intersection of the four major roads leading to the town's gateways, it was regarded as the hub, if not the actual centre, of the medieval town.

Much of the life of Leicester revolved around the High Cross. It was the site of the Wednesday market, also known as 'the townsman's market', where locals brought and sold everyday goods such as eggs, dairy and country produce. Proclamations were issued from the ancient stone cross that gave the area its name, while the street that bisected the area, High Cross Street, was the most fashionable in the town, home to the best houses and the best inns.

On this day, the town council passed a resolution for the construction of a new monument to adorn the area. The plan was to mark the site with 'a cross or market house to be made and erected and built this summer'. The new building cost £100 and acted as a shelter on market day. Octagonal in shape, with pillars supporting round arches, it was topped with a cupola. Its one surviving pillar was moved to Leicester marketplace in 1884, when the Saturday market and Wednesday market were finally combined.

17 February

Up until this date, any power held by Leicester officials was strictly under license from the Crown. This was because the mayor and burgesses were not recognised as having a legal status in their own right and so were unable to act independently.

This all changed on 17 February, when the petitions of Leicester's burgesses, the Earl of Huntingdon, Mr Parkins the recorder and Richard Archer (a bailiff) finally paid off and the borough of Leicester became free from the Crown and a corporation 'in fact and name' under Elizabeth I.

The incorporation made the town council official and an entity in its own right. Their offices were recognised in law and, most crucially, they were able to hold and sell land themselves, as well as sue and be sued in any court.

But, like other monarchs before her, Elizabeth was not granting Leicester something for nothing. 1589 was the year of the English Armada (a reply to the previous year's Spanish Armada) and it may be that the notoriously thrifty queen was granting the charter as a sweetener and in compensation for the costs of war. In order to hold the freehold of land for the weekday shambles, the area of the four Leicester guilds and Newarke Grange, the town council was obliged to pay a yearly rent of £137 13s and 7d.

4 November

Leicester has suffered from a number of outbreaks of bubonic plague during its history. But a document written on this date shows how much the town was suffering on this occasion – sick and healthy alike.

The plague broke out in September and the town council was quick to act: Leicester was essentially quarantined. Its inhabitants were banned from leaving and few were allowed in. This probably stemmed the spread of infection, but it also retarded business. The town quickly began to suffer economically as trade and markets ceased and people ran out of money.

A report of the town dated today showed just how desperate the situation was. Out of twenty-one houses visited, twenty were infected with plague, with an average loss of between one and five people per house on this day alone. The report also stated that there were between 500 and 600 people within Leicester unaffected by the plague but unable to work, and therefore on the verge of destitution; they had sold all they owned and faced beggary and starvation if the town could not support them.

And the town could not, for it was costing £20 a week to send out watchmen to tend to the sick and keep them isolated, as well as maintain those unable to work. Leicester was in danger of bankruptcy.

1 May

Leicester was reluctant to embrace Puritanism, despite the ruling Hastings family's attempts to persuade the town. Henry Hastings began to encourage Puritan preachers to visit and to attempt conversions – a privilege for which Leicester had to pay itself. While the people tolerated this nuisance on their streets, they did not take to having their traditional revels forcibly denied them.

May Day was regarded by Puritans as frivolous and pagan, but it remained popular in Leicester. So the Puritan population decided that if the people could not be persuaded to abandon it voluntarily, they should to be forced. In 1603, May Day fell on a Sunday – a double affront to the Puritan mind – and as the people of Leicester began to enjoy their traditional revels, which included morris dancing, the authorities moved in.

But all did not go well. The Mayor of Leicester, James Ellice, reported how town stewards were outnumbered by a 'confused multitude of base people' who had set up 'many maypoles' made from wood stolen from Henry Hasting's own estates! When the authorities attempted to stop the revels, the people resisted.

So strong was the feeling against this Puritan intrusion that the whole town of Leicester became a cauldron of unrest. Its people roamed the streets, many armed with guns, and the town remained unsettled for two more weeks.

3 February

Local gossips had always believed that Agnes Clarke, landlady of the Blue Boar Inn, had become wealthy from money belonging to King Richard III that he left hidden in his bed at the inn when he left for Bosworth Field. In 1604, a petty criminal named Harrison stayed at the inn for three nights. During his stay, he seduced the maid, Alice Grimbold, who told him that her mistress kept a sizeable sum of money in her private quarters. Together, the pair hatched a plot to rob Mrs Clarke.

On this date, a man called Bradshaw arrived at the inn to carry out the robbery. At 10 p.m., he tied up the servants, and took Grimbold to her mistress' parlour. Clarke was already tied up, so Grimbold was given her keys and told to search her coffers for money. Here she found six or seven bags of gold and silver, amounting to between £200 and £500.

Bradshaw left Alice a portion of the loot and a promise to return, then tied her up and left with the rest of the money, killing Clarke before his departure. After the plot was revealed to the authorities, Grimbold and Bradshaw were arrested. On 25 March, Bradshaw was hanged and Grimbold was burnt alive.

31st May

On 30 May, the Royalist army arrived to demand the surrender of Parliamentarian Leicester. While the town council played for time, Leicester's defences were shored up. But at 3 p.m., Royalist patience ran out and the bombardment of Leicester's walls began.

Despite a spirited defence, by midnight the northern and western walls of the town had given way and the Royalists were within. But still Leicester did not give up. Defenders on rooftops rained shot and roof tiles on to the invaders' heads while being forced further inwards, making a last stand at the High Cross and in the churchyard of St Martin's church. Here, they only threw down their weapons when they were faced with charging cavalry.

But despite the surrender, the Royalists were determined to make the town pay for its resistance. Prisoners were stripped and maimed, egged on by the king himself. A Humphrey Brown reported at Charles I's trial that he heard the king say, 'I do not care if they cut them, they are mine enemies.'

Throughout the night, houses were attacked indiscriminately, with even women and children killed. Looting was rife, with the town's mace and seals carried off. Those members of the town committee not cut to pieces were hanged. By the end of the siege, approximately 709 were estimated dead.

4 August

On this day, Jane Clarke of Wigston Magna along with her son, Joseph, and daughter, Mary, was brought before Justice Ashby by twenty-five of her neighbours. The witnesses accused the family of harassing them through witchcraft, causing illness and even, in one case, death.

The court heard how the unfortunate victims were stricken with seizures and coughed up dirt and stones. They were tormented at night by the witches manifesting themselves in their own and animal forms. When the church failed to help them, the villagers turned to 'white witch' Thomas Wood.

The Clarkes were identified and set upon, with Jane Clarke hunted down by a mob, stripped and searched for witch's marks and then bled 'with great pins and such instruments'. As a final ordeal, the witches' 'thumbs and great toes [were] tyed fast together and were thrown so bound into the water' to see if they would float. The accused 'strove and used all endeavors to sink yet they all swam like a cork or an empty barrel'.

This, the last recorded example of a witch's swimming, brought the Clarkes to the assizes. But despite the number of witnesses, the court threw the matter out. It seems that twenty years before it was taken off the statute books, Leicester no longer believed in witchcraft.

30 September

A cheese shortage in the summer of 1766 caused prices to rocket, leading to riots in Hinckley and Shilton. Despite the best efforts of the Leicester officials, the violence and looting reached Leicester on this date.

A local cheese merchant named Pridmore had stored a consignment of cheese at his Humberstone Gate warehouse against the advice of the town magistrates. Just before the Humberstone cheese fair, he attempted to remove some stock. Unfortunately, the wagon and cargo were spotted and intercepted by local women, while others set about stealing the contents and distributing the cheese to the gathering crowds. More people followed and began to descend on Pridmore's warehouse once they realised it was the source of the cheese. Guards armed with bayonets were called, followed by a whole regiment of soldiers. They succeeded in clearing the street immediately around the warehouse after reading the riot act.

However, the threat of violence was less persuasive than the draw of free cheese. The crowds around the warehouse returned and the town officials decided that their only recourse was to impound all the cheese in Leicester in the Corn Exchange and place it under armed guard. But the only way they could disperse the cheese-hungry crowd was to promise to sell the produce openly the next day at a fixed price of 2*d* a pound.

11 September

After long delays, Leicester's newest hospital, the Infirmary, was finally opened on this day. After a dedicatory church service at 10.30 a.m., the governors and the Bishop of Lincoln returned to review the hospital's facilities. The dignitaries ended the inaugural occasion with a musical celebration in honour of the Infirmary's opening at the Haymarket Assembly Rooms. Such concerts became a firm tradition for all further infirmary occasions.

Built on the site of Chapel Close, the infirmary cost £15,000 and was the idea of Dr William Watts, who recognised the need for a modern hospital in Leicester. The initial hospital was modest, with only forty beds available. Nor was it equipped with its own water supply, which instead had to be obtained from a local brewery. The hospital was constructed in the peaceful Southfields area of the town, although – rather ghoulishly – it overlooked the area where Leicester's public hangings took place. It became customary for patients to watch the executions from their windows – if they were well enough!

However, the very poor could not have been admitted. In order to secure a bed in the hospital, patients had to pay a deposit. If they recovered and returned home, the money was returned. But if they died while still in the infirmary, the hospital kept the cash as a burial fee.

15 March

By the eighteenth century, Leicester was the centre of the Midland worsted hosiery trade, with the majority of people working in the industry. But fears were growing that improved technology would destroy many of these livelihoods.

Rumours abounded of a new type of stocking frame that could do the work of sixty men, which had been offered to two local hosiers, John Good and Nathaniel Simpson. The truth was that the frame, designed by a Scottish manufacturer, was just of a simpler design and so cheaper to make. But the workers, already faced with rising food costs due to failed harvests and frozen or falling wages, were sent into a panic.

By 9 a.m. on this day, over 1,000 people had assembled in Leicester marketplace to protest against the new machine. Initially, things were peaceful enough but at around 10 a.m. the edgy crowd was set off by a football kicked into the air and disturbances began.

The mayor quickly arrived to calm the situation, along with one of the proprietors of the new frame. They offered the crowd a demonstration of the new machine to prove that their jobs were safe, but the crowd seized the machine and pulled it apart, parading the pieces through Leicester. They only dispersed when they were given solid promises that the machine would not lead to job cuts.

28 March

By 1774, Leicester was undergoing a process of modernisation and this meant that parts of the ancient town were destroyed. Amongst them were remnants of the town's medieval walls: its four ancient gateways, described by the *Leicester Journal* as 'monuments of gothic barbarism', simply had to go. Similar in design to the magazine gateway at the Newarke, they were no longer practical in eighteenth-century Leicester. Too low and narrow for modern coaches and carts to pass through, they were, according to the *Journal*, 'so narrow a foot passenger meeting a carriage went in danger of life'.

But rather than simply demolish and dispose of them, the town mayor, Mr Drake, had a much more economical solution. An auctioneer by trade, he decided that the corporation should sell them off. So an advert was placed in the *Leicester Journal*, announcing the intention to auction off all four gateways as building materials on this day at the Three Crowns Inn.

Local auctioneer James Bishop sold each gateway as a separate lot. The corporation was clearly eager to be rid of them as quickly and cheaply as possible, because part of the condition of sale was that the buyer had to take them away within six weeks, and at their own expense.

17 May

Anti-French sentiment hit fever pitch in Leicester on this date when a paroled French prisoner of war named Soules accidentally shot John Fenton, son of the landlady of the Green Dragon Inn.

The previous day, Soules had lost 6*s* to the deceased's brother, James, in a billiards match. Soules could not pay and a heated argument ensued. The following day, Soules accosted Fenton, accused him of insulting him and demanded satisfaction, producing a pair of pistols. Fenton was not prepared to fight and fled to his mother's inn – with Soules in pursuit. While James avoided him, his brother John attempted to throw the Frenchman out. But during a scuffle between the two, Soule's pistol went off, shooting the publican in the neck.

Soules fled but was arrested by the constables. This probably saved him from a lynching at the hands of enraged locals, such was the feeling against the crime and its perpetrator. But despite the coroner's jury bringing in a verdict of wilful murder, a grand jury at Leicester Guildhall only found the Frenchman guilty of manslaughter. Soules was pardoned and freed. The people of Leicester were 'bitterly dissatisfied' with the verdict – but not as much as the Fenton family, who recorded the miscarriage of justice on John Fenton's gravestone in St Martin's churchyard.

29 April

Today, the corporation 'ordered unanimously that ground not less than six yards nor more than ten yards in breadth of gallow-field, from that gate leading into the land in the occupation of Mr William Watts by the side of the south east hedge to the gate leading into the Turnpike Road beyond Harborough Turnpike be appropriated for a public walk'.

The new pathway – Leicester's first pedestrian-only path – was to be named 'Queen's Walk'. Running along the line of the old Roman road, the Via Devana, it divided private land on one side from corporation-owned land on the other. The corporation agreed to pay for the labour to build the path and to provide gravel from the town pits, while £250 for trees and shrubs were to be raised by private subscription.

On the face of it, the corporation was very generously providing the people of Leicester with a quiet and safe country walk between the town's Welford Place and the open fields of Southfields. But it had another motive. The construction of the walkway opened up the possibility of further developments in Southfields area, which is exactly what happened. In 1806, the town's new racecourse opened at the top of the walkway. This was not the only change, for the path was now more appropriately known as 'New Walk'.

1 December

Hand spinners working from home were the only suppliers of yarn for the hosiery trade in Leicester at this time. This often made supply uncertain. But a solution was at hand.

John Coltman, a local hosier, and Joseph Whetstone, a master wool comber, had formed a partnership with Joseph Brookhouse, the inventor of a machine which applied Arkwright's principle of cotton spinning to wool. It was their aim to produce a machine that would spin wool more steadily and efficiently.

The venture was based in Market Harborough, probably because of fears of a repeat of the events of 1773. The businessmen were justified in this, as their machine did pose a real threat to spinners' livelihoods. But in the meantime, they tried to talk the hand spinners round, holding talks with them and extolling the benefits of the new machine. The spinners were not convinced, however. At about 11 p.m. on this date, John Coltman's house on Shambles Lane was attacked, as stones were thrown at the windows. The Coltmans fled and the mob proceeded to Whetstone's property, where the wool comber's stock was destroyed before he too retreated.

As in 1773, the mayor attempted to calm the situation. This time, though, he failed: the Riot Act was read and the mayor received a serious, later fatal, head wound. And so began a week of bitter riots.

17 April

The French Revolution was the perfect excuse for the British government to condemn liberal principles. But they began to look for liberal scapegoats too. Today, one liberal victim in Leicester, bookseller Richard Phillips, was sentenced to eighteen months in the borough prison for selling seditious material.

Phillips was a notable progressive radical. Not only did he run a bookshop but he was also the founder of the *Leicester Herald*, the local literary society and the town's first permanent library. In December 1792, James Jackson, a journeyman shoemaker, appeared in Phillips' bookshop requesting *Rights of Man* by Thomas Paine and *The Jockey Club*, which the assistant promptly sold to him.

In January 1793, Phillips was called before a court in Leicester to answer charges of selling seditious material. Although he claimed he did not realise that the books in question were classed as seditious (and that he had stopped selling them immediately after he found they were), the court found him guilty. Sentencing was adjourned until this date so that Phillips could make a case of extenuating circumstances. He claimed to have been set up and that, despite the books in question being widely available elsewhere in Leicester, Jackson had been paid by William Heyrick, the town clerk, to buy them from his shop. Phillips' pleas were ignored.

27 October

This date was an important day for the people and businesses of Leicester, as the first canal boats reached the town.

Until the 1792 Leicester Navigation Act, Leicester was unreachable by water. But the addition of a canal had made the River Soar navigable, connecting the town to Yorkshire and the Potteries via the River Trent, and Liverpool via the Trent and the Mersey Canal. This meant that goods could be transported quickly and more cheaply.

On the evening of 26 October, two boats from Derbyshire and Coleorton left Loughborough for Leicester, laden with coal. They arrived at the Belgrave Gate Wharf in Leicester at midday today, greeted by the Leicester Navigation committee, a band and a cheering crowd of onlookers.

The committee boarded the Coleorton boat to address the crowd about the many benefits for Leicester. The principal advantage, they stated, was coal. This could now be transported more quickly and easily, meaning a drop in prices. Leicester was to see the cost of coal drop from 1s per cwt to 7/8d – a distinct advantage to businessmen and householders alike.

After a ride further down the waterway, the committee disembarked and headed back to the Three Crown Inn for celebrations. The two boats, emptied of coal, returned up the canal refilled with wool and other Leicester goods.

17 April

In November 1816, James Towles was hanged for his part in a raid on the factory of a Mr Heathcote of Loughborough. But he went to his death without naming the rest of the gang. In January 1817, however, a stockinger named James Blackburn was caught poaching. He injured the gamekeeper who arrested him and, knowing he faced the noose, immediately turned King's evidence and admitted his part in the Loughborough raid. He also named the other thirteen members of the gang.

One of those men, named Burton, joined Blackburn in giving evidence against his fellow Luddites at the Leicester Assizes. The machine breakers were greatly feared, not only for the physical damage they caused but also the social unrest. The guilty verdict, therefore, was almost a foregone conclusion. Of the eight men tried together, two were sentenced to transportation and the others to the gallows.

On this day, those six men – William Withers, Thomas Savage, John Amos, Jos Mitchell, John Crowther and Rodney Towles, the younger brother of the gang leader, went to their deaths. At noon, they were led out of Leicester prison, 'fine looking young men in the prime of life, health and vigor', according to the *Leicester Journal*. A sympathetic crowd of 15,000 had gathered to watch the men die, showing their solidarity by singing hymns with them as they walked to the gallows.

17 July

Frustrated by Leicester's lack of rail lines, local businessman William Stenson and landowner John Ellis (a friend of George Stephenson) joined together to plan and build Leicester's first railway. The 16-mile line was built to transport goods and passengers between Leicester and the mining village of Swannington.

It was on 17 July that the first 11-mile section of the railway was opened between Leicester and Bagworth. Leicester's first station at Westbridge was decorated with flags and banners bearing the words 'cheap coal and granite', 'warm hearths and good roads' and 'may the triumph of science prove the blessing of the people'.

At the opening ceremony, the directors of the new railway seated themselves on boardroom chairs in goods wagons as they prepared for the line's first train journey. As a band played, other guests joined them, sitting on planks or standing. Once everyone was aboard, a small brass cannon fired and the train set off for Bagworth.

The journey was not uneventful. The train became stuck in the Glenfield tunnel and the fine clothes of the ladies and gentlemen were soiled with smuts, necessitating an unscheduled stop at Glenfield Brook so the guests could clean up before their luncheon at the end of the line. No doubt they were deeply regretting that the first passenger trains would not run until the next day!

11 August

At 9.30 a.m. on 10 August, 21-year-old bookbinder James Cook was hanged for the brutal murder and dismemberment of John Paas. After his apprehension at Liverpool while trying to escape, Cook could only have expected to hang for his crime. But he must have shuddered when he learned that, as an extra punishment, his earthly remains were to be displayed in a specially made gibbet.

Once Cook was dead, his body was returned to Leicester prison overnight. His head was shaved and tarred to preserve it from the elements. The next day, he was redressed in the respectable black coat, waistcoat and white trousers he had worn to his death and his body was fixed into the iron gibbet. The gibbet was then taken to land along Saffron Lane, near the Aylestone tollgate, and hoisted on to a specially built, 33ft-high gallows.

Cook's execution had attracted a crowd of 30,000 and 20,000 attended the fixing of his gibbet. But the crowd's ghoulish pleasure was short-lived. Residents from the area were so disturbed by the body and the attention it was attracting that they petitioned for it to be swiftly removed. Three days later, Cook's body was taken down and buried on the spot. He was the last man gibbetted in England.

29 January

The Municipal Corporation Act of 1835 changed the way that members of Leicester's corporation were elected. The old system had been an oligarchy, where departing members of the council nominated their own successors. But on 1 January 1836, for the first time in centuries, the people of Leicester elected their own councillors.

The composition of the council was completely changed, with only four of the old members holding on to their seats. Buoyed by the changes, the newly elected borough council decided to indulge in a little spring cleaning. Previously, it had been traditional for each newly elected mayor to donate a gift of silver to the town treasury. This, along with Leicester's ceremonial regalia, constituted quite a hoard. So the councillors decided to auction the lot off.

Today was the first of six days that saw the auction of the treasure in the town's Guildhall. The notable sale of the day was Leicester's great mace, the symbol of the mayor's authority. It was brought by a Mrs Laughton, wife of the landlord of the George III Inn in Wharf Street. The landlady of the George paid £85 for the mace, which was proudly displayed in the inn. Thirty years later, the corporation repented their hasty decision and bought the mace back – for exactly the same price.

10 February

Leicester's policing had, until this date, always been rather ad hoc. Divided into twelve wards, the town was patrolled by five nightwatchmen and seventy-five informal 'day' police, responsible for keeping the streets of the town safe – with varying degrees of success as burglaries and street crimes were frequent.

Reorganisation was needed and that came with the formation of the Leicester Borough Police Force, which was modelled on London's Metropolitan Police. Incidentally, Leicester's first Inspector, Frederick Goodyer, had been one of the Metropolitan force's first officers.

Goodyer was joined by five full-time sergeants and fifty constables, who had answered adverts in the *Leicester Chronicle* on 9 and 16 January. On this day the new mayor of the recently reformed Leicester corporation, Thomas Paget, a local banker and ex-MP, swore them in.

The new officers were split over thirty-one new 'beats' established by Goodyer. The sergeants were paid £1 1s 6d a week while constables took home 18s a week. Each was supplied with a rulebook based on the London police model and a uniform consisting of a blue tailcoat, top hat, truncheon and a rattle to summon assistance.

The fourteenth-century guildhall was also modified to serve as Leicester's first police station. Three cells were added for prisoners, and quarters were added to house Inspector Goodyer.

5 July

On this date, Leicester was selected as the departure point for the world's first package tour – to Loughborough. This rather modest trip was the brainchild of cabinet maker Thomas Cook, who then lived and worked in Market Harborough. Cook was a member of the Leicester Temperance Society and it was while he walked to one of the society's meetings that he had the idea of the trip.

The extension of the Midland Counties railway was the source of Cook's inspiration. It occurred to him that this would be the perfect way to transport his fellow society members to a temperance rally at Southfields Park, Loughborough.

Cook's idea was well received. He contacted the railway to organise transport for a large party – another first, as Cook's train was the first privately chartered excursion train offered to the general public. Finally, the 540 temperance campaigners packed into eight open third-class carriages (with no seats) for the journey. Each paid 1s, which covered their rail fare, the cost of a brass band to entertain them on the journey and tea and buns at their destination – all provided by Cook.

The trip was a great success; so much so that it inspired Cook to try others. 'Thus was struck the keynote of my excursions,' said Cook, 'and the social idea grew upon me.'

19 August

In August 1842, hunger and mass unemployment led to a month of strikes across the North and the Midlands. In Leicester, Thomas Cooper, the Leicester Chartist leader, took to lecturing crowds of the discontented. The strikers from the mines and stocking trade took to the streets, parading with banners and flags and urging others to join them. Meanwhile, the authorities, who were busy swearing in special constables and preparing the yeomanry, monitored events.

It was on this date that hundreds of aggrieved stocking makers congregated at Humberstone Gate. The hosiers were only working for half a week, but still had to pay their employers a whole week's rent for the use of their knitting frames. Some of the speakers addressing the crowds shared Cooper's revolutionary views and began to urge the people to arm themselves.

Stirred up by the speeches and their own anger, the people mobilised and began to march out of Belgrave Gate towards Loughborough to join ongoing riots. Finally, Leicester officials acted. The yeomanry, accompanied by Chief Inspector Frederick Goodyer, was quickly after them. The troops drove the strikers off route and towards Mowacre Hill, where they prepared to defend themselves. But the potential bloodbath never happened. When the yeomanry charged, the workers fled to avoid massacre. The fright also seemed to break their resolve, for soon after, they returned to work.

16 February

The Shrove Tuesday Fair at the Newarke was a long-established Leicester tradition. People could browse the stalls and stock up on delicacies such as oranges and gingerbread before the frugality of Lent began. But at 2 p.m. a bell would ring and anyone of a delicate disposition was well advised to clear the area, for now was the time of the Whipping Toms.

No one knows the origin of the custom, but a group of men with cart whips would assemble, with license to use those whips on persons of any social class left within the fair. Anyone remaining was wise to pay to be left alone or else take a beating. Many chose to pad their lower legs, as this was the only place the Toms were supposed to strike. But this was not always the case. A favourite custom of the Toms was to drive victims between two lines, beating them indiscriminately. The whole event often became rather heated, leading to brawls.

This probably explains why many campaigned to have the custom abolished and, in 1846, an Act of Parliament abolished Leicester's Whipping Toms. But on this, the first Shrove Tuesday following the Act, the Toms made one final attempt to uphold their ancient tradition before they were forcibly suppressed by the police.

19 June

By the nineteenth century, Leicester had grown considerably, as people flocked to work in its burgeoning industries. But the increase in population put a strain on the town's facilities – not least its burial grounds. By the 1840s, Leicester's seven church-yards and seventeen chapel burial plots were overflowing, leading to serious public health issues as the run-off from graveyards polluted the water supply.

A new burial area was needed, preferably away from the occupied centre of the town. In 1843, the Unitarians acquired seventeen acres of land on Knighton Hill, overlooking Leicester. The land was intended as a graveyard for Unitarian dissenters but the borough took it over and acquired parliamentary permission for funerals and burials, so that it could be used to meet the urgent needs of the town as a whole.

On Tuesday, 19 June, over 3,000 people gathered in the rain at the opening ceremony of the new cemetery. The Duke of Rutland's Yeomanry Band played as the Mayor of Leicester, William Biggs – the very Unitarian who originally brought the land for his own religious group – declared the burial ground open.

The cemetery may have been ready, but no burials were made on its first official day. That did not happen for another nine days until James Page, a local hosier, became the first person to rest in Welford Road cemetery.

3 March

Today, an event occurred that revolutionised the shoe industry and allowed it to really take off in Leicester. Thomas Crick was a Leicester shoemaker with premises in Peacock Lane. He was already the only wholesale shoemaker in the town, but he was seeking to go further.

He had an idea to 'improve the manufacture of boots, shoes, clogs and slippers' which would allow them to be made more quickly and economically. Today, Crick received the letters patent for his idea.

The usual way of manufacturing footwear was to stitch soles to uppers by hand. Crick's idea was to use rivets instead, working from the outside in, rather than from the soles upwards. Crucially, this riveting would not be done by hand, but by machine – 'a very important step towards factory production' – which would allow shoes to be mass produced.

Crick's idea helped the shoe industry in Leicester to develop and expand from one solely designed to meet local needs to a manufacturing industry to rival the hosiery trade.

21 December

Today, Leicester became one of the first towns to offer a municipal water supply, when piped water was re-established for the first time since the Romans. The water of medieval and early modern Leicester was supplied by the River Soar, Willow Brook, wells and rainwater cisterns, with the later addition of a local conduit which carried water from a spring near St Margaret's church to the marketplace.

But in the rapidly growing town, the wells risked contamination from seepage from cesspits and the overall water supply was inadequate. Town officials quickly realised that the present arrangements were damaging to the overall health and sanitation of Leicester's population.

In 1846, the Leicester Waterworks Company was set up and in 1847 an Act was passed which allowed the construction of a reservoir at Thornton, 7 miles from Leicester. But Leicester Waterworks was unable to raise the capital it needed. So the borough council agreed to provide £17,000 of the required £80,000.

Eighty acres of land were purchased and a dam built to create a reservoir for 333,000 gallons of water. The water was filtered at a works built on the site and piped to Leicester. On this day, the first of that water reached the town, with the Temperance Hall the first building to receive it.

25 July

Today, Leicester citizens witnessed their last public hanging, as local man William Brown was hanged outside the Welford Road prison. Nicknamed 'Peppermint Billy' after his father's occupation as a mint maker, Billy had just returned from a ten-year sentence in Tasmania for horse theft. Within a month he was charged with the murder of the Thorpe Arnold toll keeper and his young grandson. A tobacco stopper and a pistol of the type used by Australian bushrangers were found at the scene, along with bloodstained items of Billy's clothing.

Billy was found guilty, despite protesting his innocence. The Society of Friends tried to obtain a reprieve based on hearsay that Billy was certified insane in Australia, but no evidence could be produced.

So, after a good night's rest and a large breakfast, Billy met his fate in front of a crowd of 25,000 spectators and a squad of 150 police. He approached the scaffold calmly and, despite promising to do so, made no speech or statement. William Calcraft, who was paid £10 to come from London to do the job, hanged him. As the trap opened, Billy's father, who was watching from one of the best seats in the nearby Turk's Head across the road from the scaffold, was heard to say, 'Well done, Billy. Tha's died a brick.'

7 January

Secularism, or 'the religion of humanity', is the belief that the concerns of this life and not the next are of primary importance. Leicester had a long tradition of secular pioneers from Richard Phillips, the founder of the town's first permanent library, to Thomas Cooper, the chartist. So it was natural that the town should be the home of the world's first secular society.

In the 1850s *The Reasoner* advertised regular Sunday evening meetings of the society at No. 148 Belgrave Gate. But it was not until today that a motion was passed, forming an organisation called the Leicester Secular Society. The meeting in question – the society's first official one – was held in the Russell Tavern on Rutland Street, chaired by Mr W. Holyoak, a leading secularist. The tavern was agreed as the regular venue for society meetings every Sunday at 6.30 p.m. (It would be some twenty years before the society had its own secular hall.) The subscription for members was set at 1*s* per quarter and twenty-two members initially enrolled.

After the motions were carried, the meeting set about its main business: celebrating the birthday of Thomas Paine, the Anglo-American author of *The Age of Reason* and political activist who inspired America's Declaration of Independence, and a revolution in freethinking and human rights.

18 July

By the nineteenth century, the East Gates area of Leicester was a pedestrian's nightmare. Five major roads – Gallowtree Gate, Humberstone Gate, Belgrave Gate, Churchgate and Eastgates – converged to form a junction where the constant flow of traffic meant that it was a struggle to cross the road safely.

What was needed was a point of sanctuary. So the corporation decided to create an 'island' at the crossroads, replacing unsightly storehouses for the nearby haymarket with an elegant new monument.

On this day, the scaffolding was removed from the 'Haymarket Memorial Structure' just in time for the Royal Agricultural Show. The tower, designed by Joseph Goddard, was impressive. Built from Ketton stone and Mountsorrel granite, it stood between 30 and 40ft high, with a platform of 18 sq ft.

There was one problem, however: it wasn't complete. The tower was supposed to be decorated with four statues of Leicester notables: Simon de Montfort, Thomas White, William Wyggeston and Gabriel Newton. Unfortunately, the statues were unfinished and not in place on time. Even the choice of subjects caused muttered complaints, as of the four, only Wyggeston and Newton were born in Leicester. But despite the inauspicious start, the clock tower (as it became known once its clock was installed) quickly became a favourite local landmark, replacing the High Cross as the centre of modern Leicester.

25 March

In 1847, a Mr T.P. Clarke, a cotton-reel manufacturer, opened a set of private baths along Kings Street and New Walk. The baths were fed with spring water and heated with waste shavings from his factory. They were known as the Tepid Baths.

In 1846, the 'Leicester Improvement Act' had authorised the corporation to provide bathing facilities to the general public. But they did not build their own. Instead, they approached Clarke and, in 1849, began to pay him £100 of his yearly expenses – on the condition that he opened the baths to the general public. A 100ft-long, 3–4ft-deep public bath was therefore built, which charged 'per penny, per person, per swim', earning the baths the new name the 'Penny Baths'. This constituted Leicester's first public bathing facilities since the Romans – beating even London in the provision of these facilities.

It was on this date that the corporation formally took the baths over from Clarke, becoming his tenants for a rent of £500 per year. The change in management led to a change in terms. Children were now allowed to use the facilities at half price – as long as they brought their own towel. Women were also given their own exclusive, but rather restricted, bathing time: between 8 a.m. and 12 p.m. on a Tuesday.

7 August

At 7 a.m. on this grey, drizzly day, church bells rang across Leicester to celebrate the opening of the new town hall. Until this point, all civic and legal duties had been conducted in the town's medieval guildhall which served as a council chamber, police station and court. But in the words of its senior magistrate, Dr Shaw, Leicester's 'increased requirements' caused by its expansion meant 'an enlarged sphere'. A more 'magnificent building' was now required.

The day began with a ceremonial farewell to the guildhall as the town council and city magistrates sat for one last time in the old building. Then, they assembled outside with the police, ancient lodges, leading tradesmen, lamplighters, fire brigade and city dignitaries to begin the journey to their new home.

Shops and buildings were decked out with flags and huge crowds turned out to watch the procession travel to Horsefair Street. The mayor unlocked the gates of the red-brick, Queen Anne-style town hall and addressed the crowds from the balcony. Leicester then celebrated in style.

While officials enjoyed a dinner at the Corn Exchange followed by a ball at the Assembly Rooms, the rest of Leicester marvelled at the grand firework display at Victoria Park racecourse. The festivities concluded at 10 p.m., when the 145ft town hall clock tower was illuminated with limelight.

23 October

The telephone was a modern apparatus experienced by the few rather than the many in Victorian Leicester – until this day in 1877. A resident of St Richard's Road and telephone enthusiast, Mr J.T. Gent, decided to put on a display of the new-fangled instrument for the general public at the Emmanuel church Sunday School.

Mr Gent began his display by explaining to the packed hall of fascinated onlookers the theory behind the workings of the telephone and how it was transforming life in America. A *Leicester Mercury* reporter was thrilled to note that the telephone had allowed conversations between people as far as 37 miles apart! Mr Gent then showed off a range of telephones that he himself had made – the first phones to be publically displayed in Leicester – before moving on to the main event: the demonstration.

The telephones in the hall were connected by 1¼ miles of wire to similar apparatus in the nearby factory of Messrs Harris. The connection was made to the factory and people in the audience were invited to try out the phones themselves. They were amazed to hear not only the voices of the people in the factory down the receiver, but also the sounds of them singing songs and playing musical instruments.

22 April

Cricket became an important sporting pastime in Leicestershire in the eighteenth century, with the first mention of a cricket match being in a notice in the *Leicester Journal* in August 1776. A few years later, Leicestershire and Rutland Cricket Club was formed. Players began to regularly take part in matches against other clubs – some local, such as Nottingham, and others as far afield as Marylebone.

But the club lacked a suitable venue. Matches were usually played on Victoria Park, but the cost of enclosing the cricketing area for games was overly expensive. So the cricket club began to look for a suitable, permanent home.

In 1877, 16 acres of ploughed land were purchased from the Duke of Rutland at Aylestone Park. Here, at a cost of £40,000, a dedicated sports complex was constructed. It consisted of an athletics ground, a hotel for visitors, and the cricket pitch, which took up 12 acres of the overall ground.

The new ground was initially known as 'the Aylestone Ground' but it was quickly renamed Grace Road. Many believe this was after famous cricketer W.G. Grace, but it was in fact named in honour of a local landowner.

This day saw the new ground's first match between the Leicester Eleven and a visiting Australian team, the 22 Colts. The Eleven won.

29 May

In 1876, the corporation purchased a low-lying area of meadowland on the east bank of the River Soar, which they turned into a new public park. The tender went to William Barron & Sons, one of the most famous gardening firms in Victorian England. Slowly, the meadowland was transformed into 40 acres of gardens, complete with bandstands, summerhouses and a lake. The new park was named Abbey Park, for the ruins of Leicester Abbey opposite.

Today, the park was officially opened by the Prince and Princess of Wales (the future Edward VII and his wife Alexandra of Denmark) – the first time royalty had opened any institution in the borough. The occasion and fine weather drew crowds from around the county. After a reception with the mayor, the royal couple processed through Leicester to the new park, stopping off in the marketplace on the way, where 6,000 children charmed them by singing the prince's hymn.

Not so charming was an incident when a drunken man accosted the royal carriage, insisting the princess shake hands with him, although he was quickly hustled away by the police. But the day was not spoiled. At the park, the lady mayoress presented the princess with a silver spade on behalf of the ladies of Leicester, which she then used to plant a young oak to commemorate the occasion.

23 March

In 1867, the Vaccination Act allowed local authorities to prosecute dissenters against inoculation. Leicester had always managed its outbreaks with quarantine and many believed improved sanitation, not injections, were the way to eradicate disease. But, in accordance with the Act, the corporation began to prosecute, issuing 6,000 summonses which resulted in sixty-four committals to prison, and homes sold to meet costs and fines.

On this day, opposition reached a crescendo when several thousand people held an anti-vaccination demonstration in Leicester. National groups gathered alongside Leicester's Anti-Vaccination League at the Temperance Hall before processing through the town to a rally in the marketplace.

Around 700 banners featured in the procession, with messages such as 'parental affection before despotic law' and 'better a felon's cell than a poisoned babe'. The banners were accompanied by a number of floats. A child's coffin was carried in one, described as 'another victim of vaccination'. Others contained 'furniture seized for blood money', representing belongings sold for fines. One even contained a gallows and scaffold from the county goal, for the symbolic execution of Edward Jenner.

Banners of support hung from buildings and cries of approval from the gathering crowds showed that the league represented the majority of Leicester's population. By the time the procession had reached the marketplace, between 80,000 and 100,000 people had gathered to hear the speeches.

22 February

Competition from local Hinckley hosiery firms forced Leicester employers to price more competitively. To do this, wage cuts were proposed to the hosiery unions and a level of reduction was agreed upon.

But on the 8 February, lists were posted showing a huge variance across Leicester. Workers faced cuts of between 5 and 60 per cent of their wages, depending on who they worked for. Only workers at the famous N. Corah & Sons escaped reductions. Smaller employers, however, felt that the decrease in wages were essential to their survival.

Approximately 1,000 people in the worst-hit factories immediately left work and over the coming days, the situation worsened. By 11 February, large crowds moved through the town 'howling and hissing', eventually attacking the factories and warehouses of the offending employers.

The corporation stepped in to mediate and the strike ended on this day, when employers and unions reached a compromise solution. The agreement had important ramifications for industrial relations in Leicester for years to come, as it went far beyond the initial grievance. Instead of being reduced, hosiery workers' wages were revised. Working conditions were also improved, and employers gave the unions assurances that they would not seek to cut costs by employing boys instead of men and that no man would have to operate more than one machine at a time.

5 January

On this day, Leicester awoke to the heaviest snow of the winter. But rather than prompt many to stay in bed, 'the storm found work for many men who would otherwise have been unemployed'.

Men began clearing pathways and roads for a few shillings. Others, many of whom could not reach their usual work, answered the summons of the borough to help clear the town. The gangs cleared snow clogging the town centre, transporting it to Belgrave Gate, Welford Road recreation ground and pits off Regents Road. Thanks to their efforts, by 10 a.m. many footpaths were clear and around half of the town's trams were back in operation.

The snow also brought amusement. At 9 a.m., a crowd watched the futile efforts of a Black Maria at Leicester prison. The van was taking prisoners to the quarter sessions, but came to a standstill after only 100 yards because the horse baulked at the snowdrifts.

Officers failed to coax the animal, so the local fire brigade's horse, 'a very strong and willing animal', was summoned but was ultimately defeated by the slippery road and weight of the vehicle. A horse from the London and North Western Railway Company finally succeeded in moving the van to 'the applause of a considerable crowd', and it reached the town hall at 10 a.m. – half an hour before the final court official arrived.

8 March

In 1881, the Improvement Bill gave Leicester Corporation the power to build essential flood defences to protect the town and its outlying regions. The corporation invested £85,000 and work began.

Unfortunately, it was not completed in time for the heavy rainfall of March 1889. On this day, after days of substantial rainfall, a further 1¾in fell in a twenty-four hour period. The rain dislodged timber sleepers being used in the cutting of a new river channel in Bede House meadows. They were washed downstream by the water and caused a blockage that resulted in the very flooding they were supposed to prevent.

Low-lying streets in Leicester's west end were flooded. By 3 p.m., streets off Oxford Street and Aylestone Road were waterlogged and the cellars of Messrs Kemp & Sons in Mill Lane were so severely flooded that the factory was forced to close.

By 6 p.m., residents of Mill Lane and neighbouring streets were taking refuge in upstairs rooms as, according to the *Leicester Daily Mercury*, 'the streets themselves assumed the character of canals'. Milk carts, bakers' carts and high-wheeled vehicles were mustered to transport stranded residents to the safety of higher ground. At the same time, the Midland Railway was submerged between Thurmaston and Syston, with passenger lines covered and part of the embankment giving way.

31 August

A six-day taste of the Wild West began in Leicester today when Buffalo Bill's Wild West Show, billed as a 'Representation of Indian and Frontier Life' arrived at the town's Belgrave Road Leicester Cricket and Bicycle Ground.

The manager of the show, Major Burke, quickly arranged the twenty-two buffalos, 200 horses and mules and 250 people – seventy of who were genuine Native Americans – into two camps of 'Cowboys' and 'Indians'.

Two performances were given each day at 3 p.m. and 8 p.m. in all weathers. It cost 1s for open seats and between 2 and 4s for seats under canvas. Visitors were also allowed to explore the camps before the shows and discover how real cowboys and Indians lived. The Indians were a source of particular fascination, with the *Leicester Mercury* noting that they spoke very little English; hence their habit of saying 'how' rather than 'how do you do?' Many were allied Sioux Indians, but others were hostages or prisoners allowed out on license.

Two of the most famous Indians in the troop, Kicking Bear and Short Bull, fell into this group. While the *Mercury* had favourably described most of the Indians as looking 'intelligent and in most cases good natured', they were rather less sure of Kicking Bear, describing him as 'a scalp hunter to the backbone'.

16 September

Welford Road and Leicester Tigers are synonymous. But it was not until today that the Tigers made the ground their permanent home. The club had until this point leased ground at Belgrave Road, but when they came to renew the lease, they found that the terms had changed unacceptably. So they began to look for a new home. Eventually, they came to terms with the corporation, signing a ten-year lease on a parcel of land sandwiched between Welford and Aylestone Roads.

Not only was its position on two major roads perfect for the club, but the new ground was near the town centre. Permission was received for the ground to be 'artificially levelled and drained' and work promptly began, at a cost of £200.

In all, £1,100 was spent on preparing the new ground – a considerable sum for the times. The club placed adverts in *Athletic News* to advise the public of the new arrangements and this date was chosen for the ground's grand opening, when the Tigers played their first match.

The game was against Leicestershire XV, which saw a victory of 17–0 for the Tigers – an auspicious start. Following the opening game, the new ground's facilities were much admired. But there was one criticism: a railing was needed to keep the playing area clear of spectators.

9 November

Leicester proved itself quick to pick up on new fashions from the capital when, just six months after the first cinema screening in London's Leicester Square, a moving picture show was put on in one of the town's theatres.

The venue was the Empire Theatre of Varieties in Wharf Street. The Empire occupied the site of the Gaiety Theatre, the music hall where Joseph Merrick, Leicester's Elephant Man, had once appeared. Although only three years old, the Empire followed in the Gaiety's footsteps by providing the people of Leicester with the latest in variety acts.

The theatre staff put up bills proudly proclaiming this latest entertainment innovation as 'Animato Scope – the first appearance of this marvellous show in Leicester'. But the show was not a cinema screening as we know it. Rather than a movie, theatregoers were treated to a series of short films of real-life activities. Features included 'Waves Dashing over Dover Pier', 'The Emperor of Germany Reviewing His Troops', 'Yarmouth Fishing Boats in Full Sail' and 'Niagara Falls'. Nor would the showing have been able to keep the audience entertained for hours; each roll of film was about 80ft in length, meaning that a film only lasted for around one minute and twenty seconds.

7 February

The streets of Leicester were filled with a riot of good-natured patriotic fever in the early hours of this morning, as the Leicester Yeomanry departed for the Second Boer War. The soldiers, all volunteers, had trained at the Magazine Barracks where they were billeted. They were due to leave Leicester railway station at 4.30 a.m. – a suitable hour for a low-key departure.

But at 11 p.m. on the 6 February, the departure of the soldiers became the focus of the town's drinkers. Instead of going home at the end of their evening, they began to gather around the barracks. By 2.30 a.m., a cheerful crowd had gathered despite the cold, singing songs and cheering. By 3.15 a.m., nearby Newarke and Oxford Streets were densely packed and torch-lit. Someone had delivered a mechanically charged piano and others had strung up Union Jacks. 'It seemed as if all of Leicester were up,' commented the *Leicester Daily Mercury*.

The street party was still going when the yeomanry left the barracks at 3.30 a.m. The crowd followed them to the station, increasing as it progressed until it lined the route so thickly that people had to climb lampposts to get a view. By the time the soldiers reached the station, rockets were being let off and the raw recruits were seen off by an estimated crowd of 15,000 people.

2 May

Today, Leicester sacrificed the remains of one of its grandest medieval buildings and 'one of the most prominent features' of its High Street to progress. The Lord's Tower, or Huntingdon's Tower, was the last of two towers that had once flanked the entrance of the grandest medieval town house along Leicester's High Street.

The house was originally built in 1500 for Richard Reynolds, a local merchant. By the Elizabethan period it belonged to Henry Hastings, 3rd Earl of Huntingdon, who used it as his Leicester town house. The house took up much of its side of the High Street and in its time had played host to Mary, Queen of Scots, James I and Charles I.

It was the removal of this last fragment of the house, along with neighbouring buildings, that allowed the High Street to be widened. Firstly, the recent brickwork was dismantled, revealing the original stonework and casement windows. After this, the tower was deconstructed storey by storey, as knocking it down as a whole was likely to be dangerous.

But despite the careful demolition and the building's picturesque appearance, there were no plans to re-erect the tower elsewhere. Instead, the newly revealed building was photographed for posterity and the ruins investigated for any relics of its past.

12 May

Today another long-standing Leicester tradition ended when the last fair was held at Humberstone Gate. The fair had been part of Leicester's life since 1473, when Edward IV granted the right to hold a fair on a strip of ground to the south of Humberstone Gate every May and Michaelmas (29 September).

The fairs were opened by a ceremonial procession of the mayor and burgesses and proved popular, their attractions ranging from the unusual to the exploitative. One fair in 1795 was described as showing exotic animals such as zebras and kangaroos alongside sword swallowers, fire-eaters and 'Irish giants, dwarfs [and] armless ladies'.

But by the late nineteenth century, the fair was beginning to be viewed as tawdry. When its end was announced, the *Leicester Guardian* expressed only the smallest regret that such an ancient Leicester tradition had to end, as this was far outweighed by the relief of being rid of something that had 'annoyed us for so long'.

The fair, despite its ancient pedigree, was an anachronism, according to the paper; no longer relevant or wanted. It simply had not evolved along with the people of Leicester, who were now better entertained by the modern conveniences of theatres, music halls, concerts, libraries and excursions, rather than the exhibitions of monstrosities and 'unintellectual amusements'.

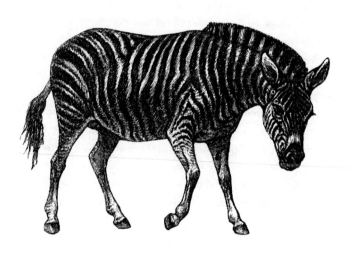

18 May

For some time, Leicester had been preparing to replace its horse-drawn trams with a new electrical tram system. Old tramlines were torn up as the new lines were laid down, while the horse-drawn trams continued alongside the work. It had meant months of disruption to the town, but on this day, the first new trams finally began to run.

A reception was held for 300 special guests at the town hall, after which twelve horse-drawn trams took the party to the new power station on Painter Street. There, the power for the new system was ceremoniously switched on for the first time and the party – taken on a journey from the power station to the new tram depot at Abbey Park Road – became the first people to travel in the new electric trams.

Their experience did not end there, for they transferred on to three decorated trams which made a special tour of the lines around Belgrave and Stoneygate, before their journey ended at the New Walk Museum.

It was not until 7 p.m. that members of the general public were allowed to try out the electric trams. Despite the late hour, there were plenty of takers, with the vehicles packed to capacity.

4 June

On this day, 500 unemployed Leicester men gathered in the marketplace to set off on a march to London to petition King Edward VII. Politicians were ignoring the issue of male unemployment and charitable donations only paid lip service to the problem of 'thousands of workless, foodless and joyless men existing in the midst of plenty'.

By noon the men had assembled in the marketplace, with thousands of spectators. Many of the men were disabled ex-soldiers, some with legs missing but still determined to make the journey to London. The Revd Donaldson gave a brief service and addressed the crowd about the necessity of the march.

At 12.30 p.m., the men began their journey, led by Amos Sherriff and George 'Sticky' White, the secretary of the unemployed committee. The town band accompanied them and at the head of the procession was a banner proclaiming: 'Leicester Unemployed, march to London, representing 2,000 men, women and their families.' The traffic in Leicester was brought to a standstill, with roads only clearing once the march was on its way.

The *Leicester Mercury* applauded the marchers but feared they would do little good. It was wrong. Although the king refused to see them, a vast crowd greeted them in Trafalgar Square and the marchers' efforts helped expedite the Unemployed Workman Act.

11 April

The people of Enderby were rather surprised when the first balloon voyage across the North Sea ended in a local field on this day.

The balloonists were Dr Kurt Wegener, a leading aeronaut of the day and record holder for the longest balloon voyage without descent, and a Mr Koch. They had begun their journey at 8.15 p.m. the previous evening from a suburb in Berlin. It was never their intention to achieve this ballooning first; their original destination had been France. But winds had driven them onwards to the coast and then across the sea to England.

By 11.15 a.m., they had reached the Wash but the wind drove them onwards. By mid-afternoon, they were near Leicester and found they could finally descend. At 3.15 p.m., curious villagers spotted the balloon over fields near Enderby Hall and went to investigate. They were in time to see the basket of the balloon tear through a hedgerow, pitching the balloonists unceremoni-ously to the ground before landing on top of them.

After the villagers rescued them, Mr Johnstone, the owner of the hall, invited them to stay for tea but as they were 'somewhat dishevelled by nature of their descent', they politely declined and stayed instead at Leicester's Grand Hotel before heading home the following day.

15 April

The loss of the unsinkable *Titanic* shocked the world, but for two Leicester families the grief was more immediate as they lost loved ones in the disaster.

Widower John Richardson and his son and daughter all died that night. Richardson had been an elastic web weaver who had lived at Oak Street in Humberstone Gate and worked at Bruce & Sons in South Wigston. But his health was poor, so that Easter, he had left his employment and booked passage in third class on the *Titanic*, sailing for what he hoped would be a new life in America. Richardson's body was never recovered, while his children were among the fifty-three children from third class who drowned.

The fourth victim was businessman John Denzil Jarvis, a 47-year-old second-class passenger from The Crest, Stoneygate. A managing partner in Wadkin's Engineering Company, Jarvis was on a trip to the United States with special pattern-making equipment.

Jarvis' body was also never recovered, although his wife and two sons did erect a memorial stone to him in the shape of a large black cross in the churchyard of St Mary Magdalene in Knighton. This memorial to one of the *Titanic*'s victims remains today.

13 April

Today at Leicester's Trade Hall, Leicester Labour MP and future prime minister Ramsay MacDonald spoke about the way forward for Britain after the First World War.

Even though peace was still some two years away, the meeting was already preoccupied with thoughts of an 'economic war' against Germany, with some believing it to be justified, while others decried it as 'unchristian'. MacDonald was more pragmatic. He described Britain as economically 'exhausted' by the war and argued that it was essential to rebuild quickly if Britain was not to 'fall back' further economically.

Controversially, MacDonald suggested that it made more sense to work with the Germans than penalising them as part of any potential peace. 'Why talk nonsense in order to prove … patriotism?' he asked. Like it or not, he noted, the Germans had a wealth of talent in the fields of science and medicine – something Britain would be wise to utilise, especially as after the war, current allies would become economic rivals.

MacDonald ended his speech by stating that the right people needed to be held to account in the event of victory, and that while the Kaiser and his staff were fair game, the German people were not. The British working man, he warned, could not punish his German equivalent without hurting himself.

22 April

Today, thirty-nine engineers from Leicester firm Messrs Gimson & Sons brought their case for release certificates before Leicester Munitions Court. This 'friendly action' was due to their belief that their employer was withholding said certificates.

The men stated they wanted the certificates – which exempted them from the military service that would become compulsory for all able-bodied men from 1 May – so that, they claimed, they could take on munitions work, where their skills would be more useful to the war effort.

Their representative, A. Morris, the Secretary of the Leicester and District Iron Trades Federation, said that by bringing the action he was 'carrying out practically the instructions issued by the Ministry of Munitions' to ensure that skilled men working on munitions work could not be forced into military service.

But the men's employer, Mr Gimson, pointed out that although 90 per cent of the machinery the men manufactured did go to the army, they were not as yet employed in munitions work. Despite this, he had applied to the ministry for the men's certificates – but had been told that they were receiving applications of 2,000 a day, so there would be a delay.

Gimson suggested, and the court agreed, that there would be an adjournment until this 'higher authority' decided whether or not the certificates should be issued.

28 January

By 1917, the German U-boat campaign was severely affecting the food supplies of Britain. The German High Command's decision to unleash unrestricted submarine warfare resulted in merchant ships transporting food to Britain from the US and Canada being sunk with greater frequency, leading to a shortage, a consequent rise in prices and an impending national crisis.

On this day, the *Leicester Mercury* reported the impact of the food shortages in Leicester. A meeting was called at De Montfort Hall to protest about the rising prices after three years of war. An extra source of disgruntlement amongst locals was caused by the fact that some people could better afford the increases than others. 'The dependents of men at the front and the large classes with incomes that have decreased ... find the pressure very severe,' commented the *Mercury*, adding that these were the very people also hard hit by increased taxation.

After establishing the causes, the meeting raised the question of how to deal with the problem. Rationing was one proposition, but everyone was against it. Local leaders assured the meeting that rationing would only be introduced as a last resort. Unfortunately, that last resort came sooner than expected when, by the end of the year, rationing had been introduced nationwide.

11 November

On this day, most of Leicester was quietly expecting the news of the end of the war. While the *Leicester Mercury* waited for the official go-ahead, one solitary factory in Belvoir Street had already hung out the flags.

But once the news was official, the papers were on the streets in a minute, and immediately torn from vendors' hands by eager readers. The initial reaction was muted while the town absorbed the news. But within minutes, flags began to flutter from buildings, with Granby Street and Gallowtree Gate quickly displaying all the flags of the allied nations. Within an hour, the streets were packed, with people singing, waving flags and remembering losses.

Factory workers took to the streets, with munitions girls kissing any soldiers and sailors they encountered. Someone carried a tray of half-made shells from one of the munitions factories as a sign that they would not be needed and a group of small boys bullied an effigy of the Kaiser.

At 2 p.m., the official go-ahead came for the church bells to be rung in celebration. Lighting restrictions were also lifted from the town's 5,000 street lamps. Shield paint was immediately removed from the 350 left in use during the war. But the need to conserve fuel meant that only 750 were expected to be operational over the winter.

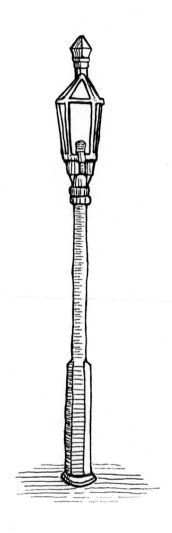

14 June

Until the eleventh century, Leicester was a city. But, when it lost its bishop, Leicester became known as a town for the next 800 years.

As the town grew and prospered, it began to petition for the restoration of its city status, without success. The last refusal, in 1907, was on the grounds that a population of 227,000 made Leicester too small to be a city. Besides, Whitehall disapproved of the public health policies of the town.

But the end of the First World War saw a change in attitude. Leicester still did not fit the minimum criteria of a population by 50,000, but on 10 June, George V visited Leicester to thank its people for their efforts during the war.

It was four days later, on this day, that the mayor, Walter Lovell, received a letter from the Home Secretary, Edward Shortt. Mr Shortt was happy to announce that 'his majesty (George V) has been graciously pleased to approve the restoration of the town to its former status as a city'.

Shortt was also at pains to emphasise that the restoration was 'exceptional treatment'. 'Leicester is of very ancient origin and appears in early days to have enjoyed the status of a city,' the letter continued. 'The proposed charter would therefore restore to Leicester its ancient privilege.'

29 June

As well as her regular and volunteer forces sent out to fight in the Great War, Leicester sent her territorial forces too. The 1/4th battalions of the Leicester Territorials reached Leicester at midnight on 28 June. But today, they reformed outside Leicester railway station as if they had just arrived and began their march through the streets of Leicester to the municipal buildings. A crowd gathered to welcome the 'Terriers' home.

The mayor and local army commanders greeted the soldiers. The mayor expressed his great pleasure at their return home, their duty done and victory won. He then recounted the Terriers' many achievements: they had helped break the Hindenburg Line, and their attack on the Hohenzollern Redoubt during the Battle of Loos – which had resulted in 3,643 British casualties in the first minutes of its final assault – had been key.

Lieutenant Colonel Dalgleish, chairman of the Territorial Forces Association, spoke of the future to the soldiers. He promised them that 'honour and glory would rest upon them for the rest of their lives' and that their children would be as proud of them as the rest of Leicester.

12 June

On this day, a court at Leicester Castle found Ronald Light not guilty of the murder of Bella Wright.

Bella had been found dead from a gunshot wound to her head on Gartree Road in June 1919. Earlier that day, she was seen talking to a mysterious man on a green bicycle who had followed her to her uncle's house. For five months, there were no leads. Then, a revolver case and a green bicycle were found in the Grand Union Canal.

Both were traced back to Ronald Light, a local man and ex-army officer. Light admitted being the man on the green bicycle. He claimed that he had accompanied Bella to her uncle's because her bike wheel was loose and he wanted to make sure she was safe. For that reason he waited for her and then cycled part of the way home with her. He denied killing her and claimed that he had only dumped his bike because of the media frenzy.

In court, no mention was made of sexual indiscretions in Light's past, allowing his defence council Sir Edward Marshall Hall to mount a masterly defence, arguing that there was no motive and destroying the credibility of two young witnesses. Locals were shocked at the verdict, convinced of Light's guilt. Perhaps this explains why he quickly left Leicester.

4 October

Leicester University began its life as the Leicestershire and Rutland University College of London on this day in 1921, when the first students began their studies.

The campaign for a University in Leicester began in the 1880s, but it was not until the end of the First World War that it gathered momentum. The day after Armistice Day, Dr F.W. Bennet opened an endowment fund of £600 to help secure the money to establish the educational facility as a memorial to Leicester's war dead.

His cause was helped immeasurably by a very generous donation from a Mr Thomas Fielding Johnson, a Leicester worsted manufacturer, who donated not money, but the premises for the university. Fielding Johnstone had purchased the buildings and land of the former Leicester mental asylum, unused since 1907, except for a brief period during the war when it served as a military hospital.

Over the next eighteen months, £100,000 in gifts followed and the dream of the college began to become a reality. Three lecturers in Botany, French and Geography were appointed and today the college's nine students were finally admitted. Sadly, renovations to the buildings were not complete, so rather ad hoc arrangements had to be made for the students. Female students, therefore, found themselves living in the old First World War nurses' huts.

4 July

Today the streets of Leicester became empty and still, as a crowd of 30,000 people gathered in Victoria Park to remember the losses of the recent war and commemorate the 12,000 lives lost from Leicestershire.

Crowds gathered an hour and a half before the beginning of the ceremony, laying thousands of wreaths of scarlet poppies, which contrasted starkly against the recently erected white marble of the triumphal arch, designed by Sir Edwin Lutyens.

At 2.30 p.m., a seventeen-gun salute from the 239th Field Battery announced the arrival of the procession of military and clergy from nearby De Montfort Hall. At a short service led by the Bishop of Peterborough, the crowd joined the choir to sing 'O God, Our Help in Ages Past' and prayed to be made 'more worthy of those who died that we might live'.

After the service two small, black-clad figures approached the monument to formally open it. They were Mrs Elizabeth Butler and Mrs Annie Glover, local mothers of fallen soldiers. Mrs Butler, who pulled the cord, had lost four of her eight sons who took part in the war, while Mrs Glover had lost three. Both were wearing their dead children's medals. Then, 'The Last Post' was played and the minute's silence was broken only by the sounds of sobbing from the crowd.

2 December

Leicester had maintained a coat of arms since the Middle Ages, when the town adopted a shield emblazoned with the arms of Robert Fitz-Parnell, Earl of Leicester. In 1343, the design was embellished when the town burgesses decided to add a wyvern. This date marked the final stage in the evolution of the coat of arms, when design updates to celebrate Leicester's restoration of city status received their letters patent.

The simple design of the shield and wyvern were now joined with a cinquefoil – a five-petalled flower symbolising hope and joy – previously part of the fourteenth-century borough seal. Two lions also joined the coat of arms, flanking the shield, which was now embellished with the helmet and wreaths from the former town's arms.

But not everyone admired the newly revamped coat of arms. Many locals felt that tigers, not lions, should have flanked the central shield, as they were the mascots of Leicester Tigers rugby club and the local regiments. In London, the College of Heralds was very snooty about it, regarding it as overly grand emblem for an upstart town while choosing to forget every element reflected part of Leicester's ancient past. As for the borough, it was completely satisfied and the new coat of arms was quickly added to corporation transport and public buildings.

26 February

'Married women not wanted' was a headline in today's *Leicester Mail* when it reported that Leicester Corporation had voted against allowing married women to work for them.

A motion had been raised that no married woman should be debarred from permanent employment for which she was qualified, simply because she was married. Marriage should not hamper the 'dignity and freedom' of women to 'select their employment', said a Miss Fortley, who raised the issue. She was seconded by a Miss Frisby, who added that the council had been inconsistent in the past, allowing women to do some jobs and not others.

But the arguments from other council members – both male and female – were weighed against the two ladies. One councillor stated that allowing women to work for the corporation would 'result in a good deal of disarrangement as business duties must necessarily clash with home duties', while another argued that such a ruling would lead young girls to become 'little drudges' who would be kept working after marriage to keep the home together.

But the final reason for the dismissal was that one good income in the home should be enough – making the matter all about money rather than personal freedom and satisfaction – and conveniently dismissing the role in the workplace taken up by women during the recent war.

5 April

Leicester, like every major city in Britain, was burdened with slums. In 1902, Joseph Dare, a pioneering Unitarian Social missionary, condemned Leicester's slums as 'insanitary and evil smelling' as well as 'nurseries of vice, disease and death'.

The immorality of slum dwellers compared to other householders is questionable. What is clear is that they were certainly disadvantaged by the cramped and insanitary living conditions. But, after the First World War, there was a sudden trend towards 'homes fit for heroes' – decent houses with modern conveniences. The slums, therefore, had to go.

Initially, many slums in Leicester were modernised as a quick way to meet the demand. It soon became clear, though, that it was better to clear them away altogether. The scheme to start clearing the slums was approved by the corporation in 1929, but the city council had to wait until it gained new legal powers under the 1930 Greenwood Housing Act to begin.

On this day, the bulldozers moved in and the first slum residents moved out of 235 houses along Green Street and Sandacre Street, exchanging their old accommodation for smart new houses on the freshly constructed Talby estate. As an added bonus, old neighbours found themselves living next door to each other on the new estates – not to retain the community spirit, but rather as an administrative convenience.

13 July

On this day, thousands of people gathered in the bright July sunshine to witness the opening of Leicester's very own airport at Braunstone Firth. The Minister for Air, Sir Philip Cunliffe, opened the event but the star turn of the ceremony was an air display by twenty-five RAF planes, which thrilled the crowds both inside and outside the airport.

However, the display was not without incident. As a flight of three Furies began to land, one stalled 20ft above the ground. The plane began to drop, the tip of its right wing hitting the ground first before spinning on one wheel – right into the path of the plane landing to its right. Fortunately, the quick-thinking pilot of the second plane avoided a collision by turning his plane out of its path. However, no one took this inauspicious incident as a bad sign, for the airport couldn't fail to be a success. Its major advantage was that it was only 3 miles from the city centre. 'No other large city has its airport in such close proximity to its business centre,' boasted the airport's official guidebook.

Sadly, the position of the airport was also its downfall. Although the 534 acres secured for its development was sufficient for growth by 1930s standards, it was inadequate for a modern airport – especially one in the middle of a city.

9 March

On this day, a *Daily Telegraph* report described Leicester as 'a progressive city' and, according to the League of Nations Bureau of Statistics, the second most prosperous city in the world. So how did it earn this accolade? Employment prospects, education, facilities, the attractive and pleasant environment and the 'progressive spirit' of Leicester people were cited as the reasons for the UN's judgment. Around 1,000 different trades operated in Leicester, with knitwear and shoes chief amongst those responsible for low unemployment figures, while the city had a 'pioneering record of industrial relations'.

These industries also restricted unpleasant emissions by increasing the use of gas in manufacturing, making Leicester 'a healthy place to live and do business'. Leicester was one of the healthiest cities due to new housing and slum clearance, and the mortality rate of 12.4 per 1,000 and 64 per 1,000 for infants was well below the national UK average of 13.1 and 77 respectively.

It was also a 'clean, bright city', with pleasant residential areas. Its streets were free of litter, neat, well lit and provided with ample transport, seven secondary schools, colleges of art and technology, a university college and a police headquarters that was 'believed to be the most up to date in the country' – all paid for by some of the lowest rates in the country.

9 June

At 7.13 p.m. on this day, the mail was being sorted at the Campbell Street Office next door to the London Road railway station when the first of five parcel bombs exploded.

The first explosion happened as a parcel containing the incendiary was tipped on to the sorting desk. The sorter, Raymond Goodwin, was temporarily blinded by a flash and suffered burns to his face and hands. As he was rushed to hospital, the police and fire brigade were called. In the meantime, four more explosions occurred, thankfully with no serious injuries. A search was then organised for further bombs.

Eight were recovered, identified by their 'bold, legible handwriting' and fictitious London addresses. They all came from the same post office, where they had been collected at 7 p.m. that evening. Each package contained a balloon filled with explosives. Disposal of them was simple; they were plunged into a bucket of water.

It seems that Campbell Street was not the intended target and the explosions were premature. The London addresses on the parcels suggested that they were intended to be loaded on a train, causing a rail disaster. The bombs were soon found to be part of a growing IRA campaign in mainland Britain. Unpleasant though Mr Goodwin's injuries were, the situation could have been so much worse.

19 November

Leicester survived the war with few major bombings, compared with many UK cities. But this night saw the German's most intensive attack on the city: so severe that it became known as the Leicester Blitz.

Air-raid signals went off at around 7.45 p.m. By 8 p.m., the sky was red as bombs and parachute mines began to drop around the city centre every twenty or thirty minutes. By 9.55 p.m., the worst of the bombing was centred on Highfields, where forty people were killed and twenty injured around the Highfield Street and Tichborne Street junction.

Buses were brought up through the blackout to evacuate the residents, while hundreds more walked up London Road to seek shelter in Victoria Park. Others hid in their own private or local shelters. Throughout the night, ARP personnel worked to rescue those trapped and injured on the streets and in their houses. The premises of many Leicester businesses not involved in the war effort were also destroyed, including Lulhams, the shoe manufacturers, and the factory of Freeman, Hardy & Willis had a narrow escape.

Finally, the all clear was sounded in the early hours of the next morning and Leicester counted the cost of the night before. In all, 150 high-explosive bombs had been dropped on the city, killing 108 people, injuring 284, and destroying 255 homes and 56 industrial premises.

12 March

Today, well-known Leicester suffragette Alice Hawkins died at the age of 83. The *Leicester Evening Mail* provided a résumé of her extraordinary life.

Unlike so many other famous suffragettes, Alice was working class; a shoe machinist by trade. She became politically active as a teenager, when she quickly realised that conditions and pay for women in the industry were inferior to their male counterparts. By her early 20s, Alice, although an active trade unionist, became disillusioned with the movement as they were more concerned with male 'breadwinners'.

Then, in 1907, she attended her first meeting of the Women's Social and Political Union in Hyde Park and immediately became active in the movement, joining a march to the House of Commons to demand votes for women that very day. This led to her first spell in prison and over the next seven years she was jailed five times, serving terms in Holloway and Leicester prisons.

It was after her first term of imprisonment that she invited Sylvia Pankhurst to speak in Leicester, and shortly afterwards the Leicester branch of the WSPU was formed. Alice was the trailblazer; the only one with the courage to mount platforms to speak. She even challenged the future prime minister, Winston Churchill, when he spoke in Leicester.

9 May

'Leicester is growing up-and out!' declared the *Leicester Illustrated Chronicle* on this day, as it celebrated the sudden growth of the city in the first half of the twentieth century, prompted by old country estates becoming new housing developments.

Since the First World War in particular, huge modern estates or 'satellites' had grown up around the traditional heart of Leicester. New Parks, Evington and Stocking Farm and Eyres Mansell had all been part of private rural estates until they were purchased by the Leicester Corporation, after the Housing and Town Planning Act of 1919 gave local authorities the power to purchase large estates on the fringes of towns and cities.

Many of these estates were still growing, with 438 new houses planned for Braunstone Firth, 1,240 for Scraptoft Valley and 1,300 for Thurnby Lodge, as well as an undisclosed number at Eyres Mansell.

The new estates were described as 'idealistic' and bright, colourful and neatly appointed, with grassland and trees breaking up the houses. Each had between two and four bedrooms, front and back gardens, and were built in a variety of styles, brickwork and colour. It was estates like these that helped make Leicester the twelfth largest city in the UK and one of the top 100 most-populated cities in the world.

5 April

Today, the scourge of many a motorist hit the streets of Leicester for the first time when traffic wardens began their solo patrols – the first in any UK city outside London.

They were the idea of Leicester's chief constable, Robert Mark, who saw them as taking over a less important part of a police officer's role – allowing the police to get on with the job of catching criminals.

The new wardens were all female, with a Mrs V. Berry of St Denys Road, Evington, described by the *Leicester Mercury* as 'Leicester's number one traffic warden'. The wardens first hit Leicester's streets in March 1961, initially accompanied by police officers. This was the first time that they patrolled the streets of Leicester solo.

Interestingly, Chief Constable Mark made it clear that their main duty was to help drivers rather than persecute them with fines. The new wardens were supposed to aid drivers in streets where parking was prohibited by redirecting them to more appropriate areas. The success of the new wardens, the *Mercury* reported, would not be measured by prosecutions and tickets but the freedom of their areas from illegally parked vehicles. Having said that, the fines were still hefty: £2 each (around £34 in today's money).

8 November

BBC Radio Leicester became the first local BBC radio station in the country. But the new initiative was not without its problems – or its opponents.

During the first programme, the mayor had to reassure nervous local newspapers that the new station's purpose was 'complementary' to their own role and not in competition. In the meantime, demonstrators with placards were picketing outside Epic House on behalf of pirate radio.

But at least that protest did not threaten to halt the broadcast. Shortly before the fledgling station got underway, the police were called to search the premises after an anonymous bomb threat was received. The caller claimed to have planted a device under the radio station, timed to go off when the first programme came on air. Fortunately, nothing was found and the programme went ahead as planned, with Postmaster General Edward Short describing Leicester's radio as opening 'a new and exciting chapter in the story of British radio'.

Tribute was paid to the mayor and city council for their support of the project. But while local officials may have been pleased that Leicester was chosen as the guinea pig for local radio, the future of the station was no means certain. For while the council wanted to fund BBC Leicester locally, they were yet to find a long-term investor.

29 September

In 1972, Uganda's Asian population was given ninety days' notice to quit the country by dictator Idi Amin. Britain became an obvious destination for the refugees, as many of the displaced had British passports.

Leicester was already home to 6,000 Asians, but the city council did not want any more. So concerned was Leicester Council that it would be swamped with Ugandan refugees that it took out an advertisement in the *Ugandan Argus*, explaining why any Ugandan Asians considering Leicester as a suitable home should think again. 'It is very important you should know that present conditions in the city are very different from those met by earlier settlers', the ad advised, before going on to stress that several thousand families were already on the housing and school waiting lists and social and health services within the city were stretched to the limit.

Whether the notice was motivated by a genuine belief that local services could not cope or a more sinister motive, it had the opposite effect to the intended aim. The advert acted as a beacon, highlighting Leicester to many who had not previously considered the small East Midlands city. Out of 27,000 Ugandan Asians, 5,000 flocked to Leicester and so began the modern multicultural city of today.

10 July

The summer of 1981 was one of violence as the disaffected youth of Thatcher's Britain finally rioted. Today, that violence reached Leicester, marking the beginning of two days of clashes between police and local youths.

Unrest began in Highfields, a multicultural area of Leicester close to the city centre. The *Leicester Mercury* reported that 'police had been monitoring the situation for hours' and at 10.30 p.m., gangs of local youths charged the lines of waiting officers, attacking them with bottles and stones. The police, who had come equipped with riot shields, beat them back to the St Peters flats, where the enraged mob began to overturn cars and set them alight. Attacks on the police continued, as a splinter group of sixty people tried to force their way closer to Charles Street police station.

In the meantime, violence also broke out in the city centre as more gangs of youths gathered at the clock tower before going on the rampage through Gallowtree Gate, smashing and looting the shops and terrorising passers-by.

The *Mercury* played down the town centre violence and suggested that the perpetrators were from elsewhere. But in Highfield, the riots intensified over the next couple of nights. Unlike the situation in places such as Brixton, the unrest does not seem to have focused on race, but on the authorities.

9 October

On this day, the most visible remains of Leicester's Roman past, Jewry Wall, became protected as a scheduled ancient monument.

Its original function was lost for centuries. In the eighteenth century it was believed to be a temple of the Roman god Janus. Kathleen Kenyan, who excavated the area in the 1930s, originally believed the area to be part of Leicester's Roman forum, but the ruins were eventually identified as a public bath house built between 125 and 135 AD.

Jewry Wall itself only survived when the rest of the baths were demolished for building material in the Middle Ages because, by that time, it had become incorporated into the west wall of the church of St Nicholas. The name 'Jewry' has nothing to do with the Jews of Leicester but instead is a corruption of the word 'jurats', the title of the senior members of Leicester's medieval council, who may have met nearby.

English Heritage declared that the reason for the wall's designation was because it was '[the] only standing fragments of the Roman town of Leicester' and 'rare in being one of the largest standing pieces of a Roman civilian building in the country and has contributed significantly to our knowledge of this type of architecture … as a result of their presentation for public display, the bath house remains also serve as an important educational and recreational resource'.

10 September

At 9.05 a.m. on this day, Alec Jeffreys, a Leicester University research scientist, was in the process of closing an experiment on how inherited illness passes through families. The experiment had not been a success. But as Dr Jeffreys was pulling an X-ray film of the DNA of one of his technician's family out of a developing tank, he had a 'Eureka moment'. The scientist realised that the results had implications other than the ones he had hoped for.

The X-ray showed the similarities and differences between the genetic code of the technician's family members. Dr Jeffreys quickly noticed that these variations were significant. Some parts of the code were different enough to make them unique to each individual, whereas others showed up similarities that allowed links to be made between related individuals. Dr Jeffreys soon came to the conclusion that DNA could be used in fingerprinting.

This chance discovery was to have worldwide implications. Dr Jeffreys' discovery was to be used in solving questions of paternity and irrefutably identifying and convicting criminals who would otherwise have escaped justice.

Unsurprisingly, it was a career-defining moment for Dr Jeffreys, earning him worldwide fame and a professorship at Leicester. Moreover, this remarkable breakthrough put Leicester and its university on the scientific world map.

2 August

On this day, the gloom of the English summer of 1985 was brightened by a sunshine party in the streets of Leicester as the first Leicester Caribbean carnival parade left Victoria Park. Even the sun peeked out of the clouds to join the thousands of people who accompanied the parade of twenty colourful floats, calypso singers, dancers and steel bands on its two-and-a-half-hour journey through Highfields to the city centre.

The mayor may have opened the carnival, but it was wholly the idea and initiative of Leicester's Caribbean community, who were keen to introduce to the town some of the spirit of the annual carnivals commonly held in the Caribbean. As the chairman of the carnival committee, Elvy Marton explained that 'they were great fun and we thought it would be a good idea to bring a little bit of our culture to Leicester'.

Judging by the enthusiasm of the crowds lining the streets, they succeeded. The fun was given a competitive edge when prizes were awarded for the best float, the best band and the best dance troupe. It was a clean sweep for Leicester in the best band, the best float and the best junior float categories, but the city's luck sadly ran out in the dance category where the winners were the Star Quality Troop from Manchester.

11 June

Nigel Keith Anthony Standish Vaz, otherwise known as Keith Vaz, was elected for the first time as the Labour MP for Leicester East on this day. He had moved to the city two years previously from London, where he had initially worked as a solicitor before attempting to start a political career.

Leicester gave Mr Vaz the political success he had hoped for. He was convincingly elected to his seat, with a majority of 1,924, and he has retained it ever since, with his greatest majority of 18,422 during the general election of 1997.

This day may have been the first time Mr Vaz was elected to parliament and the beginning of a long political career. But it also marked a number of other firsts, for both him and Leicester. His election meant he was the first person of Asian origin elected to the House of Commons since 1922, when Shapurji Saklatvala sat in the House. He also became the youngest Labour Member of Parliament at that date. But he was also Leicester's first Asian MP.

Furthermore, his length of service now means he can count himself as Westminster's longest-serving Asian member.

1 April

Leicester was an independent governing body until 1974, but changes under the Local Government Reorganisation Act of the same year meant that Leicester's corporation was no more. The city was no longer self-governing, but subject to decisions made by Leicestershire County Council.

After a twenty-three year fight, Leicester City Council finally won the right to run the city from the New Walk Council Offices rather than County Hall, when the city had its unitary status restored on this day. This meant that all key local government services – including education, social services and even refuse collection – became the city council's responsibility.

But this independence came at a price. For, although the council's leader, Peter Soulsby, urged enthusiasm for the change amongst the people of Leicester, claiming that independence would mean cheaper, more efficient services, the council faced cuts in their services in their first year due to the new authority's shortage of cash.

It seems that a shortfall in government funding meant that £17 million had been cut from Leicester's budget. The city council's staff had now swelled to around 13,000, as many former council workers moved to the jurisdiction of New Walk from County Hall. While they may have felt their future was assured by the new organisation, they now faced the every real prospect of redundancy.

28 July

Today, the future of one of Leicester's oldest buildings was assured when St Nicholas' church in the city centre was regraded as a Grade 1 listed building. The distinction, which is awarded to just 2.5 per cent of the UK's listed buildings, was made because of the antiquity of the church and its exceptional historical significance.

St Nicholas' was and is central to the history of Leicester. The small parish church is situated in what was the heart of Roman Leicester, next to the Jewry Wall Roman ruins. Constructed in 880 AD, the church is not only Leicester's oldest place of worship, but was also its former Anglo-Saxon cathedral before the bishopric of Leicester passed to Lincoln in the eleventh century. It survived sacking by the Vikings and the brutal redevelopment of the area around it when much of Leicester's medieval past was cleared away for the ring road during the 1960s.

The earliest church was constructed from masonry from the Roman baths next door. Its north and south arcades were added by the Normans and even a niche in the canopy of the north aisle began life as part of William Wyggeston's original hospital, showing that the very fabric of St Nicholas' literally encapsulates Leicester's history.

30 June

Today was the grand opening of the National Space Centre in Leicester, the UK's first attraction dedicated to space and space exploration.

Thousands of people flocked to the former brownfield site at Abbey Meadows to see NASA astronaut Dr Jeff Hoffman and British astronomer Heather Cooper open the £52 million complex, which consisted of five different themed galleries packed into the 42m-high 'Rocket Tower'. On display were space objects such as satellites, space suits and moon rock, as well as audio-visual exhibits and interactive experiences which allowed participants to deconstruct inflatable rockets, explore life as an astronaut and experience space sickness.

The centre went on to become the largest UK visitor attraction, but many were initially less than positive. Some were puzzled by the location and questioned why it was in Leicester. And in Leicester itself, many locals grumbled that it was a waste of money that the council could have spent on something different – despite the fact that only £2 million of the space centre was council-funded (the lion's share of the money actually came from the National Lottery).

But the initial visitors loved it. And the biggest draw on the opening day – for younger visitors at least – was not the ground-breaking displays and exhibits, but the chance to have their picture taken with ET.

2008

24 August

The year 2008 marked Leicester's year as the European City of Sport, a title given to reward and mark cities as European centres of sporting excellence. Leicester was the first UK city to receive the award, in honour of the city council's work in involving ethnic minorities in sport and its overall passion and commitment to city sport.

Today rounded off one of the main events of the year's 'One Great City of Sport' celebrations: Sports Fest, a seventeen-day extravaganza of sporting activity. The Sports Fest finale began on Saturday, 23 August and thousands of people flocked to the city centre to try out various free sporting activities, celebrate Leicester's sporting achievements and look to the future of British sport.

At Gallowtree Gate, a marquee was set up housing free gym and sports equipment, while at Humberstone Gate, people could try out their footballing skills courtesy of the local football associations. Other activities included breakdancing, fun aerobics and martial arts accompanied to music, while the less energetic could simply watch and enjoy the performances of stilt walkers.

The firing of confetti cannons and a live broadcast of the Olympic handover ceremony in Beijing rounded off the day at 4 p.m. Sports Fest ended with Leicester looking forward to sporting triumphs to come.

25 July

On this day, the 2009 Special Olympic Games in Leicester opened, billed as 'the biggest and most successful games' of the Special Olympics history. It was the second time Leicester had hosted the games: the only UK city to do so. Competitions in over twenty-one events were planned, right across the county.

The week-long event commenced with a spectacular opening ceremony in the Walkers Stadium – the culmination of two years of planning. At 6.30 p.m., watched by 25,000 spectators, Prime Minister Gordon Brown and his family and Tim Shriver, whose mother Eunice Kennedy founded the Special Olympics in the 1960s, the 2,700 athletes with learning disabilities began their parade around the stadium.

At the head of the parade were the Special Olympics Flame of Hope and the Special Olympics flag, carried by six East Midlands athletes. Such was the crowd's enthusiasm that the two-hour parade lasted much longer than was expected, as the sportsmen and women enjoyed the adulation they were receiving.

As darkness fell, other attractions filled the stadium. Traditionally dressed dancers from the Murpur Arts dance troupe performed a Bollywood-inspired dance routine, followed by a glowing procession of carnival animals including swans, butterflies, horses and three dragons. Finally, the Olympic flame was lit and Leicester Tigers captain Martin Johnson declared the games open.

5 May

Leicester's Lord Mayor was a largely ceremonial role, responsible for representing the city to businesses and guests. But in 2010, the Labour-controlled city council approved plans to give the city a directly elected mayor, as well as its ceremonial equivalent. The new mayor of Leicester would be responsible for the city council and all its decisions.

On this day, Leicester joined a small handful of cities across the UK when its people voted for that first city mayor, electing former council leader and MP for Leicester South, Sir Peter Soulsby. His success was categorical, winning half the first-preference votes, with his nearest opponent, Ross Grant of the Conservatives, only managing to secure 9,688.

The new mayor was voted into office for a term of four years rather than the one year tenure usually allowed to the council leader, something Soulsby believed gave him a firm basis to put in place his manifesto to secure Leicester's long-term future. Soulsby promised to spend as much time as possible out and about, listening to the 'hopes and ambitions' of the people of the city. In his acceptance speech he promised to work with all parties to create a 'confident and wealthy' Leicester. 'I am determined to hit the ground running and it will not be business as usual,' he said.

8 March

Accompanied by the Duke of Edinburgh and the Duchess of Cambridge, Queen Elizabeth II began her Jubilee tour of the UK in Leicester on this day. The street were lined with thousands of onlookers clutching Union Jacks, some with their faces painted red, white and blue. Some of the most determined and devoted spectators had made sure of prime positions by camping out nine and a half hours before the royal party arrived by train at 11.29 a.m.

Leicester was chosen as the starting point for the Jubilee celebrations because of its central position in the country and because its ethnic diversity made it the most representative of modern Britain as a whole.

The visit began with a trip to De Montfort University, where the royal party watched a fashion show. Catherine, Duchess of Cambridge, judged a shoe design competition and chose a pair of royal blue and lace shoes designed by 20-year-old student Becka Hunt as the winning entry. She was able to keep the shoes herself.

At 12.30 p.m., the royal party made their way to Leicester Cathedral for a multi-faith service. As befitted multicultural Leicester, the service included Bhangra musicians, a brass band, a Zimbabwean choir, the peal of cathedral bells and a crowd of 500 children from local schools and Scout and Guide groups.

4 February

It was on this date that Leicester University confirmed the identity of the Greyfriars skeleton found in 2012 under a Leicester car park as that of Richard III.

In front of a crowd of the world's press, university experts explained how analysis of the bones revealed an individual with a high-status diet. The remains were also contemporary with the time of Richard's death and of a person of the same age and general build as the last Plantagenet king. The skeleton was also deformed by scoliosis, which would have made the right shoulder higher than the left – enough to spark the legend of the king being a hunchback. Finally, it was announced that DNA evidence compared to living relatives of the king confirmed that the body was Richard III.

Most revealing were the details of the king's burial. Archaeological examinations of the grave revealed that Richard was buried naked without a shroud or coffin, his hands still bound in front of him, in a hastily dug grave too small to contain his body without propping the head against the sides.

After the conference, attendees were invited to view the king's skeleton on the premises of Leicester University, where it lay 'in state' in a glass case, attended by a security guard and members of the chaplaincy of Leicester Cathedral.

Bibliography

Books and Records

Bailey, Brian, *The Luddite Rebellion* (Sutton, 1998)

Beazley, Ben, *Leicester Then & Now* (The History Press, 2007)

Beazley, J.B., *Wartime Leicester* (The History Press, 2004)

Biggs, J.T., *Smallpox at Leicester* (Vol. 69)

Cavendish, George, Weller, Samuel and Wittingham, Charles, *The Life of Cardinal Wolsey*, Vol. 2 (Chiswick Press, 1825)

Cheney, C.R., (ed.) *Chronologies* (1981)

Chinnery, G.A. (ed.), *Records of the Borough of Leicester Vol. 5: Hall Books and Papers 1689–1835* (Leicester University Press, 1965)

Copy of an extract of information laid against Jane Clark of Wigston magna and Joseph and Mary her son and daughter in the case of witchcraft, held at the Leicester assizes, August 1717

Ellis, C., *History in Leicester* (City of Leicester, 1969)

Farmer, S., and Hands, D., *The Tigers Tale: Official History of Leicester Football Club, 1880-1993* (Polar Print Group Ltd, 1993)

Green, S., and Wilshere, J.E.O., *A Short History of Leicester Markets and Fairs* (Leicester Research Services, 1973)

Gould, Frederick, *The History of Leicester Secular Society* (1900)

Henry of Knighton's *Chronicle*

Hewitt, F., (pub.) *Chronologies 1885. Chronological table of Events in Connection with the Borough of Leicester*

Hinks, John, (ed.) *Aspects of Leicester: Discovering Local History* (Warncliffe Books, 2000)

Williams, David R., 'Cinema in Leicester 1896–1931' (Heart of Albion Press, 1993)

Leicester Airport memorial pamphlet (1937)

Leicester Chronology No. 1 (Pamphlet Vol. 29)

Newitt, Ned, *The Slums of Leicester* (JMD Media Ltd, 2013)

Potts, G.R., 'The Development of New Walk' in Brewin, A.E., *The Development of Leicester*

Records of the Borough of Leicester: Being a Series of Extracts from the Archives of the Corporation of Leicester, Vols 1, 2 & 3

Simmons, Jack, *A View of Leicester* (Leicester University Press, 1974)

Simmons, Jack, *Leicester and its University* (Leicester University Press, 1957)

Specification of Thomas Crick AD 1853, No. 542

Storey, J., Bourne, J. and Buckley, R., (eds) *Leicester Abbey: Medieval History, Archaeology and Manuscript Studies* (Leicester Archaeology and History Society, 2006)

Storey, John, *Historical Sketch of some of the Principle works and undertakings of the Council of the borough of Leicester … With a complete list of mayors … and head officials etc.* (British Library: Historical Print Editions, 1895)

Storey, John, *Opening of the Abbey Park by Their Royal Highnesses the Prince and Princess of Wales* (Borough of Leicester, 1882)

Thompson, James, *The History of Leicester in the Eighteenth Century* (Forgotten Books, 2013)

Thompson, J., *The History of Leicester: from the Time of the Romans to the End of the Seventeenth Century* (J.S. Crossley, 1849)

Wallace, William, *Chronologies* (1892 and 1931)

Wilshere, J.E.O., *Leicester Clock Tower 1868–1968* (1968)

Newspapers

Leicester Advertiser
Leicester Daily Post
Leicester Herald
Leicester Illustrated Chronicle (1856–1979)
Leicester Journal (1810–1881)
Leicester Mail
Leicester Mercury (1874–)

Also from The History Press

LEICESTERSHIRE

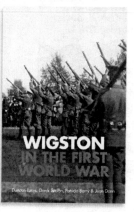

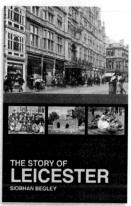

Find these titles and more at
www.thehistorypress.co.uk

Also from The History Press

GREAT WAR BRITAIN

Great War Britain is a unique new local series to mark the centenary of the Great War. In partnership with archives and museums across Great Britain, the series provides an evocative portrayal of life during this 'war to end all wars'. In a scrapbook style, and beautifully illustrated, it includes features such as personal memoirs, letters home, diary extracts, newspaper reports, photographs, postcards and other local First World War ephemera.

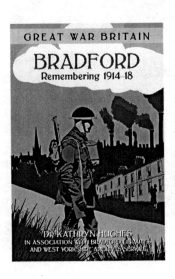

Also from The History Press

BLOODY BRITISH HISTORY

Britain has centuries of incredible history to draw on – everything from Boudica and the Black Death to the Blitz. This local series, harking back to the extraordinary pulp magazines of days gone by, contains only the darkest and most dreadful events in your area's history. So embrace the nastier side of British history with these tales of riots and executions, battles and sieges, murders and regicides, witches and ghosts, death, devilry and destruction!

Lightning Source UK Ltd.
Milton Keynes UK
UKOW03f0620250714

235742UK00001B/3/P